MICROCOMPUTERS IN TV STUDIOS

by Judith Stokes
and the editors at
Knowledge Industry Publications, Inc.

Knowledge Industry Publications, Inc.
White Plains, NY and London

Video Bookshelf

Microcomputers in TV Studios

Library of Congress Cataloging-in-Publication Data

Stokes, Judith.
   Microcomputers in TV studios.

   Bibliography: p.
   Includes index.
   1. Television—Production and direction—Data processing.   2. Microcomputers. I. Knowledge Industry Publications, Inc. II. Title.
PN1992.75.S76   1986   791.45'0232'0285   86-15243
ISBN 0-86729-131-1 (pbk.)

Printed in the United States of America

Copyright © 1986 by Knowledge Industry Publications, Inc., 701 Westchester Ave., White Plains, NY 10604. Not to be reproduced in any form whatsoever without written permission from the publisher.

    10   9   8   7   6   5   4   3   2   1

Table of Contents

List of Tables iv
List of Figures v
Editor's Note vi
Preface 1
Foreword, by William C. Hight 3
   I.   Introduction 23
   II. Results of the Microcomputer Survey 29
   III. Profiles 47
   IV. Appendixes
        Appendix A: Microcomputer Survey Questionnaire 97
        Appendix B: Directory of TV Studios Profiled 101
Glossary 107
Suggested Reading List 115
Index 119
About the Authors 125

List of Tables

Table 2.1: Profile of Survey Respondents 29
Table 2.2: Brands of Microcomputers Used 30
Table 2.3: Apple and/or IBM Ownership in Selected
            Types of Facilities........................31
Table 2.4: General Microcomputer Applications,
            by Type of Facility........................33
Table 2.5: Studio Management Applications, by
            Type of Facility 34
Table 2.6: Production Management Applications,
            by Type of Facility........................36
Table 2.7: Production and Post-Production Applications,
            by Type of Facility........................39
Table 2.8: Interactive Video-Related Applications,
            by Type of Facility........................41
Table 2.9: Software Development and Purchase Activity.....42
Table 2.10: Commercial Software Packages Owned
            by Studios.................................44

List of Figures

Figure 3.1: Deltak Inc.'s television facility staff uses IBM PCs 53
Figure 3.2: Sample page of General Foods' 1986 Video Program Catalog 57
Figure 3.3: Hobart Audiovisual Services staff members use microcomputers for studio and production management 61
Figure 3.4: Sample of a Lotus database featuring Prudential Audio Visual Department rates 79
Figure 3.5: Sample of a Lotus database featuring Prudential Audio Visual Department schedule of services 80
Figure 3.6: Sperry Corp. training department staff members working with Sperry PCs 89

Editor's Note

Of the many people involved in the preparation of this work, several deserve special recognition. Katharyn Dunham, research associate, helped a great deal during the early stages. She did extensive research before composing the questionnaire with Ellen Lazer, senior editor, Knowledge Industry Publications, Inc., and assisted in the tabulation of the survey results. William C. Hight, district manager, video development, AT&T Resource Management, kindly reviewed the questionnaire and wrote an informative, insightful foreword. Liz Harvey, copy editor, Knowledge Industry Publications, Inc., put the finishing touches on the manuscript. Finally, I would like to thank the microcomputer owners who responded to our request in *Video Manager* and the profile participants who graciously answered our many questions over the phone.

Judith Stokes
August 1986

Preface

This book is based on a survey of microcomputer use in television studios conducted by Knowledge Industry Publications, Inc. during winter 1984–85. (A sample of the survey questionnaire can be found in Appendix A.) A total of 46 usable responses was received from 17 in-house corporate studios, 15 production facilities, 5 academic institutions and 9 facilities classified as "other." The last category includes three cable access centers, two broadcast studios, one video publisher, one system design consultant, one post-production facility and one specialist in live broadcast from a concert hall.

The profiles in this book were constructed following in-depth telephone interviews with some of the survey respondents, as well as with others who did not participate in the survey but who were known to use microcomputers in interesting ways.

Foreword

The Computer and Media Management

by William C. Hight

What has happened to computers in the TV studio since the microcomputer revolution began? Why should I, a media producer and manager, be interested in computers? If I am, how can I maximize their usefulness? What do I have to know about hardware and software to become an expert? Where can I get help? Who else is doing what?

These are the questions media managers ask. I will try to cast some light upon them in the next few pages. First, some history and some theory for computer novices.

BACKGROUND

To say that the computer is a fact of life is to state the obvious. From its inception this wondrous machine has grown to the point of being applied to almost all aspects of our lives. In the beginning this power was hidden from our view because the machinery of the computing age was quite expensive, most mysterious in design and operation, and enormous.

In media we have long known that the power of the computer was at the heart of various pieces of our production equipment. We did not call these applications "computers"; we did not yet know the meaning of the word. These were "smart microchips" that strangely and mysteriously prompted our editing systems to direct our human decisions or automatically balanced the delicate interplay between light and electronics in our cameras. These brains accelerated our work, made it more accurate and began to give us more equipment flexibility and value for our money.

Intelligent microchips have not been confined to video. They have invaded our home appliances, directing operations and alerting us when the roast is done. They are in our automobiles telling us to "buckle up" or "turn off our lights," all the while busily controlling the firing of the engines under the hood. Still, all of this technology is obscured. We interact with these computers only in the sense that we operate the automobiles and the appliances, and they make things happen faster, or smoother, or better.

Time passed. Invention, redesign and miniaturization occurred. Size decreased. Power and speed increased. Cost dropped. Today these machines pervade the closest fabric of our everyday life. Today's computer, often a microchip the size of a postage stamp or smaller, equals or surpasses the capacity of a whole roomful of equipment just a few decades ago. The computer has reached the worker's desktop.

As with any form of development, a language, or set of special words and meanings, has grown up around the computer. Even as laypersons we need to have a basic understanding of the terms of the business. So, as this article progresses, I hope to increase your vocabulary. (A glossary can be found on page 107).

A final thought about today and the future. Like the equipment in our media business, the systems and applications in the computer field change and grow rapidly. This makes it difficult to stay current. I will have a few tips later on how you can attempt to do this.

"Why, as a media manager, should I be interested?" Because the computer can take responsibility for many of the highly repetitive, routine and even boring tasks that we face daily as we manage both our total operations and facilities and our specific production projects. It can make much of our work more enjoyable, more productive and even more profitable as we "manage information" through the computer. Finally, since the power of this technology is so accessible and so universal in its application, we must take the position that it can and should be used in the television medium as in so many other fields of contemporary life.

HOW COMPUTERS WORK

In its most simplified form a computer has two tasks. It is a device for the storage and manipulation of information. In our lay description we commonly think of a computer as a combination of devices, or components. The purist, however, sees a computer as only that central core of electronic circuitry that handles information storage and manipulation. This heart of the computer is called a "processor." I will use both words interchangeably to refer to the machine's brain.

The Language Barrier

Why is it taking us so long to come to grips with computer technology? Both humans and computers receive, manipulate, store, and discard information. Both can communicate information. But while each completes these tasks following its own sets of rules, it is this last process, communication, that has tended to slow the application of the computer. Basically, the delay is caused by a definite, and very observable, difference in the way that people communicate versus the way that machines, especially computers, communicate. There is a tremendous language difference at the point where humans and computers interface.

While both communicate through "language," the languages differ greatly. Though some human communication occurs on nonverbal levels, most takes place through the process we call speech. Unfortunately, and without going into great detail about the communication process, speech is, itself, an imperfect process. Consider this: first, we must use words to convey ideas and information. Words are merely symbols we use to represent information; they contain no meaning. Those who hear our words attach their own meaning based on personal experience and training. For example, when spoken, the simple English word "for" can sound like either a prepositional direction in speech, a number, or, to the sports enthusiast in the crowd, a request to duck the head quickly. We must use our experience and the conditions of the present situation to select the appropriate meaning.

The computer, on the other hand, cannot rely upon the context of the present situation to derive meaning. It must follow carefully prepared steps and sets of conditions planned in advance and placed into its memory in order to select a response. It has great difficulty dealing with the abstract and the snap decision.

The computer "thinks" in an electronic sense. Its "symbols" are minute electrical impulses occurring in rapid succession in time. In simplest terms the computer "senses" one of two electrical states, either current or no current. By stringing together a series of "on" or "off" pulses, unique codes that a computer's memory can be taught to recognize can be built. This is "machine code," the "language" of speech within the computer. Today's computer can read or process machine code at lightning speed. Machine code is, of course, incompatible with human speech and impossible for humans to understand without specialized training.

To begin to bridge this communications gap, computer programmers developed transitional languages, such as Fortran, COBOL and BASIC, to allow the translation of human speech to machine code and vice versa. While these exotic-sounding languages smoothed the human/machine interface, they are still ones that media managers would not ordinarily choose to spend time learning. English would still be the language of choice if we really wanted to communicate with the computer in a manner most comfortable and most expeditious in terms of our time and energy. Not long ago you needed the expert help of the programmer, sets of detailed instructions and considerable personal learning. Only recently have language interfaces been developed to allow us to use our own tongue. These user-friendly human interfaces include extensive use of menus and other prompts. These developments should, and do, break the computer usage barrier.

Types of Computer Systems

There are two basic classes of computer equipment or systems. First there are systems where a central computer is connected to one or more terminal devices. Many organizations have these traditional "mainframes." They are usually large machines, often housed in environmentally controlled rooms and designed to handle volume jobs for the entire organization, frequently in the accounting and financial areas. Terminals connect users to the mainframe and generally have little or no computing power of their own. You may be able to "share time" on one of these systems; however, additional programming will probably be required within the mainframe, and considerable negotiation may be necessary to secure the cooperation of those responsible for the system.

You will also probably have to learn a great deal about how the mainframe system works in order to utilize its power. You may also find the keepers of the system less than interested in your needs and experiments since their machine is used daily to perform jobs of magnitude. Further, you may find it difficult to obtain time on the machine due to large user requirements.

The second class of system is the "stand-alone" computer, most commonly referred to as the personal computer (PC). These devices have taken the world by storm. A great deal of variety exists in terms of features, price and portability. Since the PC offers users direct control over their time, use and application, I would urge consideration of the PC over the shared-time system. For the remainder of this article I will discuss the use of computing power from the standpoint of the PC.

HARDWARE AND SOFTWARE

Just what does a PC consist of? Its two elements are "hardware" and "software." Hardware is a term used to identify and classify the physical components of a computer system. As we classify a video camera as a piece of hardware, so too, a processor is a piece of hardware. Software is the set of directions or instructions that make the hardware function. Some software, called system software, is necessary to make any computer prepare itself for operation. Other software, called applications software, contains instructions to do specific tasks.

About Hardware

First, hardware. The basic hardware components include processors, display screens, keyboards, modems, printers and disk drives. As already indicated, the processor is the heart of any computer. It is a collection of various electronic circuits that actually carry on the computing. The processor also has the ability to retain or store information over time in its "memory." Memory is contained in, again, microchips within the processor.

Processors have two types of memory, ROM (Read-Only Memory) and RAM (Random Access Memory). ROM is the place where the processor stores the instructions that tell it how to conduct its basic operations. ROM cannot be changed. RAM, on the other hand, is a changeable storage area where information can be placed, recalled and replaced. The processor is a mysterious hardware element since it is kept hidden within the case of the machine.

Input Devices

All other hardware components are identified, in terms of the functional relationship they have toward the processor, as either input or output devices. They do exactly what their names imply. Input devices feed information into the processor while output devices transmit information from the processor.

Keyboards constitute the basic form of input device and come in many shapes and sizes. Although they may have special keys for special functions, they closely resemble the keyboard of the familiar typewriter ordinarily. We enter text and numeric information and instruction through the keyboard.

The "mouse" is becoming a popular input device often used in conjunction with a keyboard. A mouse is a small unit held in the hand and moved about the work surface to control the location and movement of information the processor displays on the screen, which I will detail in a moment. The mouse usually allows one or more commands to be entered by pushing buttons upon its surface rather than by pressing keys on the keyboard. The use of a mouse can greatly speed work when pointing types of actions are required, such as choosing the next function to perform or locating the next action.

Other input devices include a sensitized drawing tablet and an electronic sensor stylus. They handle the pointing types of work as does the mouse, but they also allow entry of such artistic information as structured drawings, tracings and freehand graphics.

Other input devices include scanners of one form or another. Some scanners can "read" text, bar codes or other specialized markings, or graphics and photographs. Scanners are helpful when complex or large amounts of information already exist in paper form, and reentering them using keyboards or drawing tablets would take a great deal of time. Video cameras can also be used as devices to input drawings, photographs and anything else the camera sees.

We are beginning to see systems that allow data entry through direct speech. At the moment, the vocabularies that these systems can "understand" are too limited to be useful to those of us who write for a living. As voice entry systems develop and become reasonably priced, they should find great application in the media field, particularly in scripting, since they will eliminate vast amounts of keyboard entry.

Output Devices

On the output side the display screen is the basic device. Display screens are specialized high resolution cathode ray tubes (CRTs) that present the results of input after processing. They display data from the computer's processor rapidly, virtually as calculations are completed. Although full color can be used, computer display screens generally work with a singe color, such as green or orange, for higher legibility. Originally they could only display text and numeric information. Rapid advances in this field have produced display screens that can handle complex graphic information. With many of today's display systems, what you see on the screen is a true representation of what you will actually receive as output. With some modification, regular TV receivers and monitors can be used as display screens, usually with somewhat lower resolution.

After the display screen, the printer is perhaps the most common output device, allowing us to obtain paper copies of the computer's results. Printers come with various features. Some print only text and numbers, with differing degrees of resolution and sharpness. These are known as line printers. Others can print graphics as well as text, using technologies that allow a random placement of information. For some graphics applications, particularly those requiring very large drawings, pen plotters are used. Today, highest resolution comes from a breed of laser-driven printers that deliver about 300 lines per inch of resolution. In situations where even higher resolution is required, output from the computer can be directed to phototypesetting devices with resolutions in excess of 1000 lines.

Additional Hardware Devices

Modems

Two other pieces of hardware are worth mentioning. First, modems. Modems are devices that allow computers to transmit and receive information through telephone lines. They are very valuable devices when two or more computers need to exchange information over a distance.

Memory devices

Finally, a series of devices can be used to expand the memory of the computer, the external memory devices. Since these devices have the basic task of storing information, they fulfill a dual input/output role. When stored information is fed from them into the computer, they function as input sources. They can also function in reverse when the computer outputs to them to store information for subsequent use. The rationale for having a storage device of some kind is that there is only limited RAM storage within the processor, and it must be continually modified during computer operations. An external memory expansion allows maximum continuous use of the processor memory.

External memory devices may take the form of tape- or disk-based systems. For the PC, tape systems usually use the familiar audiocassette format. Although inexpensive, tape systems are typically slow and rather cumbersome. Disk systems can be based on either flexible disks, called "floppys," or hard disks. Floppy systems usually use removable disks and generally do not have as large a storage capability as the hard disk. They are, however, less expensive. Either type of disk "drive" can be connected externally to the processor. And it is often possible to have the drive mounted within the processor's housing. I would strongly recommend at least one disk drive on any PC.

Before turning to a discussion of software, a few final words about memory are in order. Realize that a processor, in addition to manipulating information, must store data within its brain at least for short periods of time while it computes. This activity of storing and sorting requires a great deal of memory. Additional memory is used to hold the sets of instructions mentioned earlier as applications. These types of activities take place in the RAM. It is in RAM that information is stored in a systematic way; it is also where the processor can locate, change, erase and rewrite over previously stored data. You will find that most manufacturers use the amount of RAM as a measure of their basic processor size. For example, a 64K RAM computer has 64,000 individual storage locations.

As you will see in a moment, while this number appears quite large, it is small by today's standards. And, while it is not a scientific measure to say that the work that a computer can do is solely related to the size of its RAM, generally speaking, the larger the RAM number, the more you can do with the system. Today, it is not uncommon to have a personal computer with 512K of RAM or more; 512,000 storage locations is better than 64,000, but it is still not enough to handle today's business applications. This is the advantage of the disk drive. Even a small, floppy-based disk can double the RAM available. Hard disks can expand memory to 20 million locations.

Of all of the hardware mentioned, the typical PC system includes the processor with built-in display screen and disk drive, a keyboard and a printer. Additional components increase the flexibility and ability of the PC to do specialized kinds of work.

About Software

Now, software, the other half of the computer equation. I've already mentioned two types of software, system and applications.

First, we will review them and add another, "document." System software includes the sets of instructions that allow a computer to start up and bring itself to a state of readiness to do useful work. During this work, the system software tells the computer how to sequence its operations. Software of this type is often called the "operating system" of the computer in question. Perhaps the most common operating system on personal computers today is the Microsoft Disk Operating System, known as MS-DOS. Operating systems are unique to specific brands and models of computers and are purchased as an integral part of the processor. It should be noted that all forms of applications software that you wish to use must be compatible with the operating system of your particular PC.

Applications software can be defined as a program, or set of instructions, that allows a computer to do work that is directly useful to the end user. For example, in order for your computer to function as a word processor, you must install word processing application software. Applications programs to perform many different functions are available from many vendors. In the text field, there are, among others, word processors, spelling checkers, page formatters, table and chart construction sets, full publications and publishing systems.

In the art field various programs allow, for example, the construction of simple to complex graphics, animation and 3-D. And, in business, applications are available to handle various spreadsheet and database tasks, project planning and management, decision making and accounting, to name but a few. Then there are many applications for scientific and educational purposes, as well as games. The manufacturer of your computer will probably have many applications packages available for your purchase. You can also buy separate applications offered directly from software vendors.

The last type of software is called "document." You will generate this type of software as you use your PC. When you use the word processor to generate a report for the boss, you print the report on your printer and then actually give it to the boss. At the same time you want to store the data in the report in case the boss wants to make changes or updates, or in case you want a record of what you sent. Rather than storing a printed copy, you store the report as a file or document. You then give this file a special name so that you can find it again, and place the document somewhere in the RAM memory of your system. You may choose to store the document in the processor's RAM; however, because this memory is used continually by the computer each time you "run" an application, you quickly run out of space. Therefore, more often than not, if you have a floppy disk system, you save the document on disk.

You may set up a different disk for each major area of your work activity. For example, you may want a disk for all communications with your boss, another for all of your other correspondence and another for your monthly production reports, as well as others. You may have different disks for different applications, such as word processing or spreadsheets.

THE COMPUTER IN MEDIA

We now come to a discussion of your potential use of the PC. There are at least three ways in which your PC can be used in the video department. They include uses that involve the general long-term and daily operation of the total facility, uses that relate directly to a specific job in the production process and uses for which the PC is regarded as a device to control a finished product. We will summarize each area and then look at some specifics.

General Business

The computer can be applied in a global way to business problems that the media department faces, including the development of annual budgets and the tracking of results in this area. We can also employ the machine to handle daily word-processing chores, such as general correspondence, memos and the ever popular special report. We can design aids that allow us to track any number of operations, such as monthly expense or income, equipment maintenance histories, and staff and facilities scheduling.

Specific Production

You can use the PC to tackle the administrative detail connected to individual video production jobs either for management of the job or for actual production development. In management, the PC can be used to handle bids, billings, resource scheduling, talent and crew. It can be used in the development of the script and all of the related documents that follow, including scene breakdowns, call sheets, "day out of days" charts, and production and shooting schedules.

Further, we know that character generators, special effects generators, image manipulators, editors and graphics/animation workstations are nothing more than specialized computer systems that have been given sets of instructions designed to accomplish specific and very narrow tasks. A PC can be modified through hardware and software enhancements to function as some of these devices do, for character generation or graphics input and/or manipulation, for example.

Media Control

Finally, in the area of controlling interactive video situations, computers are being used to join text data, audio data, and video still and motion data in ways that allow the user of the device to receive information in a self-paced mode.

WHAT ARE MEDIA PEOPLE DOING?

We will now discuss more specifics about media applications, particularly in relation to general business and individual production. As mentioned, PCs require applications software in order to function. Fortunately, a great deal of software is available "off the shelf." The applications that you will want first will include word processing, spreadsheets and database management. While a few software programs on the market have been designed specifically for the media field, there are many others of a general nature that can be used with little, if any, modification. And you do not even have to be a programmer to use them. I will mention some sources and some tips on buying at the end of this article. First, however, I will present some of the ways that the PC and appropriate software can aid the video manager in departmental activities.

General Correspondence, Memos and Reports

Word-processing software offers a powerful way to create, store and print text-oriented data. Thus, general letter and report writing can be greatly assisted. Many word-processing programs allow the combination of more than a single data file. This feature automatically merges a file containing, for example, a standard letter with a second file containing an address list. The result is a series of letters addressed to many persons. Clearly, this is a valuable tool for marketing and communications. Perhaps the greatest asset of the word processor is the flexibility it gives you to change or edit your material. Revisions no longer necessitate rewriting or retyping. Simply make your changes electronically when you are sure you have them right. Naturally you can make a paper copy with your printer if you feel more comfortable editing in that fashion or when someone else must spend time reviewing your draft work. Some word-processing software has a provision for spelling checks and output to a variety of printing devices, including letter-quality or full typesetting machines.

Script Generation

Word-processing programs used in this application allow you to enter text and revise it rapidly. You can also use this type of program to develop initial program objectives followed by script treatments and actual scripting. Script drafts can be revised and reformatted quickly. Cutting and pasting are done electronically. The output of final materials comes in many forms, including those useful in teleprompting equipment. You should be aware that the typical video multicolumn script format is very difficult for a word processor application to handle. The problem is that word processors tend to be written to handle multiple columns along print publishing lines. When a change is made in column one, the effect is spilled directly over to the second column. In scripting, we would like to be able to treat each column independently with changes in one column unaffected by changes in the other. At the same time, we need to have some way to tie the columns together so that the visual directions line up with the place in the

16   MICROCOMPUTERS IN TV STUDIOS

audio copy where they are required. Instructions of this complexity drive word processors crazy. You may end up having to make many corrections to get the word processor to follow your multicolumn work, especially during revisions. The effort will still be worth it because of the application's speed at other scripting tasks. However, new word-processing products that overcome this limitation are now entering the market.

Filing and Retention

Once text files are created, they are stored magnetically on your floppy disk, hard disk or tape subsystem. This reduces the need for paper files. Retention is as secure as traditional videotape storage, and search and recall are rapid. To ensure safe retention, it is a good idea to make duplicates of more valuable files; these duplicates can then be stored at different sites.

Scheduling and Control

Spreadsheets allow you to record the application of your human and physical resources and to predict those periods of future time when you will need to develop fill-in work or arrange for increased capacity. Some spreadsheets have graphics report generators that allow the automatic creation of charts and graphs to help tell the story. These very flexible programs typically allow data that is highly numerical to be manipulated in "what if" situations.

Once initial data have been entered, a change in any individual figure (or group of figures) creates automatic recalculation of all other affected figures. From the data collected above, you can determine who is responsible for what.

Departmental Capital, Personnel and Expense Budgets

Spreadsheet and database software (perhaps even word-processing software) is of great help in developing, recording and modifying the details of business operation. Initial budget information is input and can be tracked against actual dollar commitment throughout any given time period. As a result, will you have a much better idea of where you stand. In addition, forecasts can be developed to project the status of the budget at the end of the year, and comparisons between the current time period and earlier time periods can be made.

Productivity Measurement

Database management software acts as a file manager. You will be able to measure how much actual time a project or function takes and generate many other useful statistics that can help you to plan and budget more effectively.

Internal/External Communication

Your PC can be connected to other computers through wires, telephone networks or the sharing of magnetic media. This allows you to take advantage of the electronic mail features of computer software. You will be surprised at the time saved when you do not rely on paper for messages. "Telephone tag" no longer will exist, and you will find it easy to share the details of a project as it is planned, which may help avoid costly misunderstandings and revision.

Personnel and Training Records

Possibilities abound here for individual personnel files and the tracking of training needs and results. Furthermore, data from this application are useful in the annual budgeting process.

Accounts Receivable/Payable and Billings

As with most general computer installations, your PC can record and monitor your orders, payments and requests for payment. While the organization's central computer may do the actual work, your system may be able to communicate the necessary data and thus reduce the need for more paper.

Planning

A new breed of applications programs offers sophisticated abilities to look at the discrete steps in any mangerial or production process. These project planning and management programs allow you to design a flowchart of the steps in a process, to rearrange them, and to allocate resources and add time lines. The programs also generate a variety of reports, including PERT, GANTT and Critical Path. Naturally, changes are reflected instantly throughout the charts as they are made.

Production Quotes and Proposals

Spreadsheet programs can be set up to list all of the individual factors and components in the video production. Each factor can be priced according to your established charges. Quotes for individual programs are automatically developed as you "enter" the specific quantities of each factor used for the production. Changes in any one factor can automatically revise all other related factors.

Production Budget Planning and Control

Like the quote, a spreadsheet can be developed that shows you when budgeted amounts are to be spent and record the fact that they have been committed. It is very easy to see at a glance just where you stand in terms of total or individual factor budget commitment.

Production Time Line and Scheduling Control

Spreadsheet programs can be developed to track all critical dates in the production process. In addition, you can use such programs to allocate and record the need for various types of personnel and equipment. You will be able to spot bottlenecks and shortages quickly.

Edit Decision Lists

Edit decision lists (EDLs) can be developed from the original script files in the memory of the computer as the production progresses. It should also be noted that once the script is done, including scene designations, you can create shooting schedules that group locations or talent for cost-effective production.

Production Cost Analysis

At the conclusion of the production, or at any point along the way, the data contained in your spreadsheet can be summarized to provide you or the client with a picture of the project's financial status.

Talent File

Here, the value of the database software is readily apparent. Consider the ability to electronically file names, addresses, telephone numbers, pay rates, use history and the special qualities of all of the talent you have used. Again, physical storage space is small since no paper is required. Recall is swift and can be done using any search parameter you wish. For example, you might search for all female voices having a grandmotherly sound used within the last six months.

Music/Effects/Stock Footage Catalog

Just like talent, you can establish files of available resources for music, sound effects or stock footage. Although this type of data file requires considerable time to set up the ability to search rapidly for what you need, the end product may justify the effort.

Program Logging and/or CCTV Control

If your operation includes the distribution of video by cable or some other form of transmission, the PC can be assigned to monitor and/or control the operation of the network. VTRs can be started, stopped and recycled. Program listings can be generated for either paper or electronic distribution.

Parts Inventory

An often overlooked area, a parts inventory program in the PC can control all expendable small parts. This offers a better view of supply expense than a single supply line item in a department budget. More important, you can analyze the parts usage data to determine what is used and in what volume. This information can assist you in accurate budgeting and timely placement of restock orders, which will affect the overall cash flow of the organization.

Equipment and Maintenance Inventory

This inventory program is also disregarded frequently. But if you log the equipment that you use and record each maintenance event review over time, you will begin to notice developing patterns. For example, you will be able to compare the repair history of different brands of the same type of equipment. If you do your own maintenance you will even be able to identify specific electronic or mechanical components that have poor maintenance lives.

Labels and Shipping

The labels for your products can be printed on special forms to fit into the printing device attached to your PC. Your computer can generate labels for shipment on an almost automatic basis.

Security

Although it may seem exotic, it is possible to let your PC take on some responsibilities for security. With the addition of electronically controlled locks, wiring and special software, your computer can monitor entrances and exits to your facility.

GETTING FURTHER INFORMATION

Where can you get help? Part of the answer to this question depends upon your interest level and the amount of time you want to devote to learning more about the computer. Another part relates to the type of help you are looking for. Are you trying to determine which equipment or which system to purchase? Or, if you have a system, are you interested in applications that you might use?

If you have nothing else to do for the next month or so, your sources can include extensive reading and/or formal training through seminars and short courses. If you are like most of us, the work load will prevent such intensive study and your sources should allow you to minimize the learning time and to proceed immediately. First, begin to read two or three computer periodicals regularly. (See the Suggested Reading List on p. 115.) Check your local newsstand or library and select at least one magazine that relates to the specific type of equipment that you own or wish to buy. Second, visit local computer stores and ask for demonstrations of systems and software applications. Third, seek out others who are using PCs. All of these sources can be of help either for equipment or application assistance.

If you are at the equipment purchase stage, your major concerns include price, availability, vendor support for training and maintenance, system compatibility with other local existing systems and availability of applications software to fit the equipment system. The vendor, usually a local computer store, will be your base of operations. Describe your reasons for wanting a system and ask for the names of others who have purchased for similar uses. Call some of them to find out how satisfied they have been with equipment reliability and dealer service. Try to find out how helpful the dealer has been after the sale, particularly in helping users to operate their system and its software. Comparison shop for price and availability. Finally, check the documentation that comes with the system. Is it available? Does it look complete? Does it read well? Do you understand it?

If you are already using a system and are seeking to expand its use, concentrate on the experiences of others when selecting software applications. There are also computer clubs for each of the major system brands. Clubs usually offer literature and some exchange of software. Clubs often hold local meetings and/or have online help services that you can subscribe to and can access through your modem. Local vendors and the magazines should provide club addresses. Some vendors offer demonstration packages that allow you to see the nature and operation of their software. Some allow trial usage. As with a hardware purchase, check the documentation that comes with the software. Again, does it look complete? Does it read well? Do you understand it?

A final thought about getting help. You are probably a member of at least one trade association in the media field already. Check the educational program offerings for the association's next national or regional meeting. More and more media trade associations are offering sessions related to applications of the computer.

It has been my intent to present an overview of the PC as a useful decision-making and process device for media managers. This device has the power to drastically reduce the time needed for many of your management and production functions. It will make your work more accurate, more professional in appearance and more timely. And it should save you money in the long run. However, do not mistakenly believe that PCs and their software are magic solutions to any of your needs. It is rare to find a piece of software or an equipment system that instantly meets all of your needs and can be used without some study. But I hope that the survey data that follow will place the idea of using the PC more firmly in your mind. I urge you to read critically and jump in.

Part I

Introduction

Computerization is not new to the television industry; both production and post-production hardware have utilized the technology for years. The use of microcomputers in the television facility, however, for applications ranging from scriptwriting to graphics generation, is just beginning to be explored to its fullest potential. The reasons for this are many. Only in the last few years have microcomputer prices come down low enough to put the technology within grasp of even the smallest television studio. Software specifically designed for the video industry has been slow in coming to market. But perhaps the greatest obstacle has been the disdain with which computers have traditionally been viewed by those in the "creative" fields. To those in the arts, the term "computerization" is often synonymous with rigidity—the mere thought of which a videophile finds unbearable.

But because the technology is now so available to those in all facets of business and industry—as well as to those managing their affairs at home—it has lost much of its mystique. And many in the video industry are finding that rigidity can foster flexibility. This new receptiveness to computer technology presents some challenges for those managing a television studio, be it within a corporation, a production or post-production facility, an academic institution or a broadcast operation.

GETTING STARTED

Harnessing microcomputer technology for the efficient operation of a television department requires a new mind-set. Managers are not simply buying a camera, a videotape recorder, a special effects generator or the like; they must assemble an entire system—keyboard, disk drive, monitor, printer, software, necessary interfaces and assorted peripherals—that has little to do with television yet will have a serious impact on the productivity of the facility. And this all hinges on identifying needs.

The needs analysis is often a major issue. The capabilities of a video camera, for example, are finite, because a camera has a specific purpose and can perform only a limited number of functions. But a microcomputer's potential lies in applications, and these are determined, in large part, by the person directing the computer project, the software chosen and the computer acumen of those using the system. It is no wonder, then, that a number of the audiovisual managers interviewed for this book compared working with microcomputers to the chicken-and-egg syndrome. One cannot explore the potential of a system without using it routinely on a daily basis, and it is impossible to get this informal exposure without first installing a system.

To add to this, using microcomputers is ancillary to the business at hand at a television facility. The technology is, therefore, foreign to many. Those managers who have some computer savvy themselves, can rely on knowledgeable staff members and colleagues or have a department within their company to guide them are fortunate. Those who must rely on other sources, most often video and computer dealers and reading material, are not as fortunate. Trial and error, though frequently expensive, is often the best teacher, according to those interviewed.

The majority of those interviewed were dissatisfied with the assistance they received from video and computer dealers. They found that the dealers were most interested in promoting the products they had on hand, showing little regard for the user's special needs. The managers also found that video dealers know little about how to interface computers with video hardware (such as the micro-controlling routing switcher, character generator, editor, etc.) and that they make little attempt to get the information. As one respondent puts it, "The vendors don't know how the video equipment itself works, so how are they going to tell me how to interface it with my IBM?"

Nor have those interviewed had much better luck with the video equipment manufacturers. Because salespeople and customer service representatives are seldom knowledgeable about how their hardware can be connected to a micro, users are often passed from one department to another in search of an answer. One manager we interviewed found that the hardware designers themselves—the engineers—have the answers, but they are so inaccessible to the end user, and customer assistance has such a low priority with them, that even they are not very helpful.

Clearly, the time has come for audiovisual dealers and manufacturers alike to recognize the special needs of those customers who want to use microcomputers for more than word processing and budgeting. Many in the industry have a vision of what the ideal microcomputer/video hardware relationship would be; they need just a little assistance from those marketing the products. (Some facilities have begun to explore the possibilities with great success. See the department profiles that appear later in this book.)

While facilities are receiving little support from manufacturers and dealers, their efforts to utilize microcomputers are being backed, for the most part, by upper management, although many departments reported that, at the outset, some superiors questioned the validity of the television department's use of computers. As one manager explains, "We are seen as the creative types, the ones who 'make TV'; we had to show them that our facility is really a business that needs the assistance micros provide." At in-house corporate studios, any resistance that does surface is often intensified, because television departments, in many cases, do not adopt the corporate standard in computers. Since these television departments tend to operate independently of most other company divisions, they often opt for micros that will best meet their needs, regardless of the systems being used elsewhere in their own companies.

Once objections were overcome, according to those we interviewed, management often staunchly supported the move to micros. Superiors were impressed with the higher levels of efficiency the departments achieved, especially in the areas of program budgeting and script generation. As one interviewee says, "The micros afford us more control over our operation than we ever had before."

As for applications, there are many. But as the statistics that appear later in this book demonstrate, studio and production management are by far the most prevalent. Within these areas of application, budgeting, scriptwriting and scheduling are the most common. Virtually every television facility using a micro, therefore, owns a good word-processing and spreadsheet program.

MICROCOMPUTER APPLICATIONS

While microcomputers have found their niche in studio and production management, their potential in the areas of production and post-production control and interactive video are just beginning to be realized. Though the opportunities indeed exist and some users are tapping micros for everything from editing to teleconferencing network control (see the Aetna Life & Casualty profile), these applications tend to require a great deal of ingenuity and a strong commitment on the user's part. This relates to the problem discussed earlier; inserting a disk into a drive and using a word-processing or spreadsheet program call for little technical know-how, unlike linking a micro to a routing switcher or editing deck. The difficulties are augmented because little vendor support is available.

One post-production area in which television facilities have had significant success with microcomputers is character generation. Many departments bought a micro specifically to control the Chyron VP-1 (the industry's workhorse of a character generator) and are just beginning to explore the capabilities of the computer in other areas (see, for example, the Oklahoma Police Department Training Center and Shadyside Hospital profiles). Conversely, those facilities that purchased a micro for word-processing applications are just beginning to look into computer/video hardware interfaces.

It should be noted here that in departments that have more than one micro, it is not unusual to find two, three or four different types in use. It seems that in facilities with this diversity, each micro has its own specialty and is rarely used for other applications (see, for example, the Hobart Corp. profile). One might guess that this would lead to confusion; on the contrary, the managers we interviewed for this book find the arrangement works well because it allows staff members to become familiar with various micros, and it affords the department increased flexibility.

Although the types of hardware, software and applications found at the television facilities we surveyed vary greatly, the respondents almost unanimously praise the microcomputer. The benefit most often recounted is increased productivity coupled with greater accuracy. Managers with micros feel they have more control over their departments than would otherwise be possible, because the technology allows them to see at a glance where they stand with budgets, personnel and the like. Most invaluable is the "ripple effect," according to those interviewed, who said that the micro's ability to show the impact of a line item change on the bottom line keeps operations in check. One user sums up the general consensus of the respondents by saying, "I don't know how my department functioned before we got the micros."

Managers did caution those about to install microcomputers not to underestimate the amount of time that will have to be devoted to training. Many reported that they, as well as upper management, had expected staff members to be instantly productive on the micros and had given little thought to the learning process. In short, a great deal of unproductivity always precedes the increased productivity afforded by micros.

The installation of and learning about a new computer system will nearly always interrupt and disturb the ordinary operations of a video department. When possible, setup should be scheduled to take place during slack periods, and management and staff members alike should realize that learning to use a computer takes time. In most cases, several months will pass before tasks can be accomplished more quickly on the computer than they were before its arrival.

Part II

Results of the Microcomputer Survey

During winter 1984-85, Knowledge Industry Publications, Inc. conducted a study of microcomputer use in television studios. The results of this survey form the basis of this book. Of the questionnaires mailed out, 46 usable replies were returned. (The breakdown of these responses can be found in Table 2.1.)

MICROCOMPUTER OWNERSHIP

The study shows that two microcomputer manufacturers, Apple and IBM, have almost equally strong holds on the television studio market (see Table 2.2). Apple micros are used at 21 (46%)

Table 2.1: Profile of Survey Respondents

Type of Facility	Number	Percentage
In-house corporate studio	(17)	37%
Production	(15)	33
Academic (including school systems)	(5)	11
Cable access	(3)	7
Other[1]	(4)	9
Broadcast studio	(2)	4

[1] Includes a video software publisher, a specialist in live broadcast from a concert hall, a system design consultant and a post-production facility.

Table 2.2: Brands of Microcomputers Used

Name of Brand	Number	Percentage
Apple	(21)	46%
IBM	(20)	44
TRS-80	(4)	9
Sony	(3)	7
Commodore	(3)	7
Franklin	(2)	4
Compaq	(2)	4
Other[1]	(8)	17

[1] There was one response for each of the following brands: Altos, Atari, Dec Mate, Eagle, Sperry, Tektronics, Wang and Xerox.

of the 46 studios surveyed, while IBM models are in place at 20 (44%) of the facilities that responded.

Within the Apple family, the IIe and the IIc are most prevalent, although a handful of Macintosh, II and II+ models can be found. In the IBM line, the PC, XT and AT dominate. At 15% of the studios, both Apple and IBM units are used.

IBM enjoys a slight edge at in-house corporate studios, according to the survey, which found that 47% of these users own IBMs, 35% own Apples and almost 18% own both. The two companies are on equal footing at the production facilities surveyed; IBM and Apple models are each in nearly 47% of these studios, and they coexist in 20% of the operations. Apple, in place at four out of five of the academic television studios polled, is the clear favorite in this sector (see Table 2.3).

The reasons cited most often by video professionals for choosing Apples include ease of use, reliability, low maintenance cost, moderate price and software availability. IBMs, on the other hand, are often chosen because they are the corporate standard; software availability is another strong determining factor. Apparently, the majority of departments looking forward to expanding their micro networks will opt for IBM models.

Table 2.3: Apple and/or IBM Ownership in Selected Types of Facilities

Type of Facility	IBM Number	IBM Percentage	Apple Number	Apple Percentage	Both IBM and Apple Number	Both IBM and Apple Percentage
In-house corporate studio	(8)	47%	(6)	35%	(3)	18%
Production	(7)	47	(7)	47	(3)	20
Academic	(1)	20	(4)	80	0	0

Those studios that have both Apple and IBM micros report few problems with having two different systems in operation. These departments tend to assign specific tasks to each micro, thereby limiting the types of software purchased for each and allowing staff members to become proficient at specific tasks on each micro. Many of the managers who have both the Apple and the IBM claim that the arrangement allows them more flexibility than would otherwise be possible, because each micro has its own specialty and can therefore be used to its fullest potential.

It is clear that, because of the nature of video equipment, people who work in television studios are extremely conscious of obsolescence. Managers who have gotten stuck with an editing or production system that became outdated the day before it was delivered are determined not to let the situation recur with their microcomputers.

Obsolescence has forced those who have been most successful in harnessing the technology to give a great deal of serious thought to the exact ways they would use the hardware. This involves looking not only at the video department's short- and long-term goals, but also those of the company the department serves. "Where will the company be in five years?" and "How can my department help it get there?" are basic questions that must first be answered.

Those departments that do not own an Apple or IBM microcomputer have brands that range from Radio Shack and Commodore to Sony and Franklin. Because of the varied types of micros in use, Radio Shack, which is in a scant 9% of the facilities surveyed, places third behind Apple and IBM.

Brand apparently has little bearing on product reliability, as virtually all of the video professionals reported that their micros have served them well, with few, if any, breakdowns. This confidence in the hardware is reflected in the fact that few of the studios surveyed have maintenance contracts on their micros. When a minor problem arises at a facility that does not have its own computer maintenance staff, it is more than likely to be fixed by an in-house computer enthusiast, saving the studio the 10% to 12% of the purchase price generally charged for service contracts.

APPLICATIONS

General Management Applications

It is not surprising that, in each of the sectors surveyed, studio management was the microcomputer application most often cited (see Table 2.4). This is because tasks in this area largely entail word processing, a function that is relatively simple to implement, as well as master. In fact, the majority of those surveyed originally acquired their micros specifically to carry out studio management tasks, and they are only now beginning to realize the technology's potential in other areas.

Studio Management Applications

The survey indicates that, overall, 91% of television studios are using micros for general management applications. Within this category, ranking as the top tasks are correspondence, memos and reports (80%); budgeting and/or financial analysis (78%); studio cataloging and filing (54%); labeling and shipping (52%); inventorying (50%); scheduling and control (39%); maintaining personnel records (35%); and tracking accounts receivable/payable (32%) (see Table 2.5).

Table 2.4: General Microcomputer Applications, by Type of Facility

Application	Percent In-House Corporate Facilities	Percent Production Facilities	Percent Academic Institutions
Studio management	94%	100%	80%
Production management	82	67	60
Production tasks	71	67	60
Interactive video	29	40	40

Table 2.5: Studio Management Applications, by Type of Facility

Application	Percent of All Studios	Percent of In-House Studios	Percent of Production Facilities	Percent of Academic Institutions
Correspondence, memos, reports	80%	88%	87%	60%
Budgets and/or financial analysis	78	77	87	60
Studio catalogs and files	54	65	47	40
Labels and shipping	52	53	60	60
Inventory	50	70	40	60
Scheduling	39	65	20	40
Personnel records	35	29	40	60
Accounts receivable/payable; billing	33	29	47	40
Catalog of stock footage	30	35	40	0
File and catalog correspondence	26	41	20	20
Productivity management	20	47	7	0
Electronic mail	20	18	27	20
Music/sound effects catalog	15	18	20	0
Program logging	15	18	13	20
Talent file	11	24	7	0
CCTV control	7	12	0	20
Security	4	0	0	20

Production Management Applications

Creative Tasks

Tying as the second most common applications are production management and production/post-production tasks, each carried out at nearly 70% of the studios surveyed. Production management tasks utilize, for the most part, word-processing and spreadsheet programs; the latter entails microcomputer/video hardware interfacing.

Script generation, accomplished on micros at 63% of the studios surveyed, is by far the most common production management task for which the technology is utilized (see Table 2.6). Because scripts are generally subject to lengthy and complicated approval procedures to ensure accuracy of content and appropriateness of tone and subject treatment, they rarely emerge from reviews unchanged. It is no secret that revising a script to include changes can take more time than writing the original work did.

While micros save scriptwriters a great deal of time in making revisions—because they can manipulate words, sentences, paragraphs and entire scenes with tremendous ease and great speed—users almost unanimously complained that it is difficult to work without the customary two-column audio/video format. While most scriptwriting software—as well as general word-processing programs—will output in two columns, the market is just beginning to offer scriptwriting software that will allow the writer to see audio and video on the screen simultaneously. Three of the new programs designed to meet this need are Split/Scripter from Ixion, Inc., a Seattle, WA firm, and PowerScript and Script Master from Comprehensive Video Supply Corp., which is located in Northvale, NJ.[1]

Financial Tasks

The other production management tasks accomplished most often on the micro deal not with creative elements, but with finances. These are cost analysis (35%), quote and proposal writing (30%), and budget planning and control (30%). Time line/scheduling control came in last (15%) (see Table 2.6).

---

[1] PowerScript is available through Knowledge Industry Publications, Inc.

Table 2.6: Production Management Applications, by Type of Facility

Application	Percent of All Studios	Percent of In-House Studios	Percent of Production Facilities	Percent of Academic Institutions
Script generation	63%	82%	53%	60%
Cost analysis	35	29	33	20
Quotes and proposals	30	18	27	40
Budget and planning control	30	24	27	20
Time line/scheduling control	15	12	13	20

At first glance it might seem that these figures are low, since money management is a task for which micros are ideally suited. Upon further examination, however, it is easy to see why only one third of television facilities have explored this area.

First, a significant time commitment is necessary in setting up a cost analysis/budgeting program. Rates, for everything from equipment to talent and services, must be input, as must a multitude of other variables. In addition, data must be continually updated to be of value to the user.

Second, micros often impose standardization and rigidity. In some cases, these are not desirable byproducts. In budgeting and proposal writing, managers often need some flexibility, based on their intuitive feelings about a program or equipment acquisition. Because micros cannot duplicate or allow for this, it is often difficult for users to build in fudge factors, which are purely subjective.

The third reason for the reluctance of some facilities to track finances with the micro is that doing so would require a lot of downtime as users learn how to work with the software. Unlike most word processing software, spreadsheet programs can be difficult to learn, especially if they are used infrequently.

Despite the problems, the facilities that are using micros for budgeting and other financial tasks have had much success. The managers report that their departments are more efficient than ever before and that going "over budget" is a far less frequent occurrence. The microcomputer at Federated Department Stores' subsidiary, Ralphs Grocery Co. (see profile later in this book), has given the video department a new means of control over its money flow. According to Stephen Brown, television specialist at Ralphs, the department has not exceeded budget on any project since the Calc Result spreadsheet has been in use. This, says Brown, is because the department can tell—at a glance—where it stands on each production.

Brown's experience is not uncommon. Many of those interviewed cautioned, however, that those new to such budgeting applications should be prepared to spend a great deal of time setting up the software, as well as learning how to work within the parameters of the software. Spreadsheets can be limiting in that they require categorization of data. Since video departments' ways of appropriating services and funds vary so greatly, users must be prepared to adapt budgeting software to their own needs, as well as to give up some freedoms.

Scheduling control is a less popular application because snags occur so frequently during shoots that running back to the micro to make changes is often impractical, if not impossible.

Production and Post-Production Applications

Production and post-production are other facets of television that have been touched by the microcomputer. Slightly more than 41% of those surveyed use micros for character generation, and 39% utilize them for graphics. The figures drop to 22% for teleprompting and editing and 11% for animation (see Table 2.7).

The growth of microcomputer utilization in production and post-production has been hampered by the lack of vendor support available to the facility interested in interfacing its microcomputer with video hardware. Video dealers, by and large, know little about such setups, and computer vendors know even less. Those survey respondents interviewed were unanimous in criticizing the industry for its lack of assistance in this area.

This is why microcomputers are relegated to such tasks as character and simple graphics generation. The manufacturers of character and graphics generators design them with microcomputer compatibility in mind, and they offer assistance to the buyer. The overwhelming majority of those in the survey who use their micros for character generation own the Chyron VP-1.

Though only approximately one fifth of those surveyed use their micros in the editing process, many of those interviewed expressed interest in the possibilities present in this area. The primary task for which micros are utilized is the generation of shot logs for offline editing, but there are many options in online editing as well. Again, the scarcity of vendor support is slowing growth in this area.

Interactive Video Applications

Interactive video is another application for which micros have proven valuable; 35% of those surveyed have incorporated the

Part II: Results of the Microcomputer Survey 39

Table 2.7: Production and Post-Production Applications, by Type of Facility

Application	Percent of All Studios	Percent of In-House Studios	Percent of Production Facilities	Percent of Academic Institutions
Character generation	41%	47%	40%	40%
Graphics	39	24	40	60
Teleprompting	22	18	20	40
Editing	22	18	27	20
Animation	11	6	27	0
Other	9	18	0	0

technology into this area. Nearly 24% use the technology to design interactive programs, and 19% use micros to control or present interactive programs (see Table 2.8). Because not all of those surveyed even produce interactive programs, these percentages are high, but not surprising. What better way to track the branching required in interactive programs than with a microcomputer? As for presentation, micros control programs when disc or tape players do not contain internal computers. This ranges from systems that require the user to input data on an external keyboard to those that automatically control the playback of interactive programs.

SOFTWARE

As discussed earlier in this chapter, television studios are sometimes reluctant to use microcomputers because they find it difficult to adapt their budgeting and management systems to the structure followed by prepackaged software. Recognizing this, some companies (including Comprehensive Video Supply Corp., the Bottom Line and Ixion) have, over the past few years, marketed software designed specifically for the television industry. But these are not without problems, as facilities must still work within predetermined parameters.

It is therefore not surprising to find that 38% of the 42 studios responding to questions concerning software origin indicated that they have developed their own software (see Table 2.9). Another 48% expect to develop their own software, and 7% "might" do the same.

Interestingly, of the 15 in-house corporate studios responding to these questions, 27% have developed their own software, while a substantial 60% expect to do so. Production facilities—14 of which answered these questions—have been faster to initiate programming, but fewer expect to carry through in earnest. Nearly 36% of the production facilities have developed their own software, but only 29% expect to do so.

Among the applications for which facilities develop their own software are interactive video control, teleconferencing scheduling, teleprompting, mailing label generation and shot cataloging.

Part II: Results of the Microcomputer Survey 41

Table 2.8: Interactive Video-Related Applications, by Type of Facility

Application	Percent of All Studios	Percent of In-House Studios	Percent of Production Facilities	Percent of Academic Institutions
Interactive program design	24%	29%	20%	40%
Control/present program	20	24	20	40
Other	9	12	7	20

Table 2.9: Software Development and Purchase Activity

Response	Percent of All Studios	Percent of In-House Studios	Percent of Production Facilities
Have developed their own software	38%	27%	36%
Expect to buy more software	74	67	79
May purchase more software	5	7	0
Expect to develop their own software	48	60	29
May develop their own software	7	7	0

Aetna Life & Casualty (see profile section later in this book), for example, which with IBM both owns Satellite Business Systems and operates 12 teleconferencing rooms nationwide, has managed the development of teleconferencing scheduling/control software. Termed "invaluable" by the head of the video department, Richard O'Keefe, the software enables routing switcher-linked IBM XTs to automatically control the switching and management of the network. It also provides instant status reports and work orders pertaining to the company's teleconferencing business.

As for teleprompting, several firms have devised their own PC-controlled setups. One, John Stanley Training Programs (see profile section), expects to soon make available a program that turns a script run on 3-inch-wide adding machine tape into easily readable teleprompter copy.

Another facility that has developed its own software is ViMart Corp. (see profile section), a marketing services company. Video manager Ric Getter has produced a set of the Society of Motion Picture and Television Engineers' (SMPTE) time-code calculators that significantly "improve the speed and accuracy" of back-timing arithmetic.

Since software is the lifeblood of any microcomputer system, it stands to reason that nearly three quarters (74%) of those responding to this series of questions expect to purchase additional software, while almost 5% "might" do so.

No single software package emerges as the clear favorite among television studios. This is, in large part, because the applications are as varied as the facilities are—and there are so many offerings from which to choose. Some software packages have a stronger hold on the television market than others do, and these reflect the most frequent applications (which were discussed earlier in this chapter).

It is therefore not surprising to find that the most popular programs are for spreadsheet analysis, word processing and database management (see Table 2.10). Lotus 1-2-3 has apparently found its niche in the television studio market, as it is owned by nearly 22% of the facilities surveyed. Second in popularity is VisiCalc (15%), followed by Multiplan (13%) and WordStar (11%). Capturing nearly 9% of the market are each of the following: PFS: FILE, MultiMate, dBase II and Apple Writer.

Table 2.10: Commercial Software Packages Owned by Studios[1]

Software	Number	Percentage
Lotus 1-2-3	(10)	22%
VisiCalc	(7)	15
Multiplan	(6)	13
WordStar	(5)	11
PFS: FILE	(4)	9
MultiMate	(4)	9
dBase II	(4)	9
Apple Writer	(4)	9
PFS: REPORT	(3)	7
Displaywrite 2	(3)	7
dBase III	(2)	4
PC File III	(2)	4
Fontrix	(2)	4
Magic Window	(2)	4
Appleworks	(2)	4
Profile	(2)	4
VisiFile	(2)	4
Easy Mailer/writer	(2)	4
TIM IV	(2)	4

[1] Titles owned by fewer than two studios are not listed.

Templates—software designed to be used in conjunction with other software—are another alternative for studios seeking programs customized for the television industry. While only a few templates are currently on the market, the potential exists for an array of television-specific offerings. (See the Lincoln Center for the Performing Arts profile that appears later in this book.)

CONCLUSION

The research shows that microcomputers, which were enjoyed by privileged television facilities alone just a few years ago, are now in the mainstream of the industry. They are no longer viewed as expensive toys, but as valuable tools nearly as vital to a studio's survival as cameras and VTRs.

Part II: Results of the Microcomputer Survey

Nearly all users surveyed contend that they would not be able to sustain their level of productivity were it not for their microcomputers, and they caution others that to deny the technology's effectiveness as a television management and production aid is to close the door on progress. This can prove fatal to even the best studio, since a video facility that does not move forward cannot survive in the highly competitive and creative television field.

The future for microcomputers in video, therefore, is a bright one. But it is not without problems. Perhaps the biggest obstacle is the lack of vendor support available to those in the video profession. Though many video equipment dealers are making an extra effort to train their sales force in the area of microcomputers and video, much room for improvement is still possible. Those vendors who are well versed in this area are rare, and fortunate are those clients who have found them.

Computer dealers, on the other hand, have made fewer strides in learning how the technology can best be harnessed by a television facility. For this reason, managers contemplating purchasing a microcomputer for a television studio should talk first with others who have recently installed a system, and then with video dealers who have been recommended as knowledgeable in this area. The final purchase can be made through computer vendors, but in most cases, they should not be the buyers' primary source of information.

Clearly, the lack of assistance available to video facilities has hampered the growth of microcomputers in the areas of production and post-production.

The more common and less complicated applications of word processing and budgeting can be learned with an expenditure of time and effort. But the more technical facets of television operation—such as editing, graphics generation and interactive video control—can only be microcomputer-assisted when users are savvy not only about software, but also about hardware. For the technology to flourish in these areas, it is necessary for those who have had successes with micros in production and post-production to share their knowledge. And those interviewed for this book made it clear that the industry is fortunate to have professionals willing to do exactly that.

In short, the facts indicate that a microcomputer will not turn a poorly run video facility into a well oiled machine. But it will give an organized and productive studio just the edge it needs to stay on top of its productions, its finances and its clients. The net result is that the time and energy saved can be put into the creative process. And that, after all, is our goal.

Part III

Profiles of Television Studio Microcomputer Projects

AETNA LIFE & CASUALTY
Hartford, CT

Type of facility: In-house corporate studio
Population served: Employees and trainees
Micros owned: IBM XTs
Software packages owned: Lotus 1-2-3, Displaywrite 2, MultiMate, Smartcom
Contact: Richard O'Keefe, department head

The television department at Aetna Life & Casualty, following the corporate standard for microcomputers, purchased six IBM XTs in 1984. On average, each 512K system costs between $4000 and $5000. Approximately $3000 has been spend on software.

Like many other in-house facilities, Aetna's video center uses its micros primarily for studio management applications. Six of the 21 staff members use the XTs for such tasks as scheduling, correspondence, productivity management, inventory control, and the generation of labels and shipping data.

One of the more ambitious projects under way is the creation of a database to track the more than 50,000 slide transparencies managed by the department. This will replace a paper-based filing system that has proven to be too time-consuming and sometimes less than accurate.

At present, the only facet of production touched by the micro is character generation; one of the XTs is paired with a

Chyron VP-1. The department expects to purchase graphics software in the near future and is investigating using the XTs in online and offline editing. (Aetna has a 1-inch facility.)

But two of the most innovative micro applications at Aetna deal not with studio management, per se, but with equipment management. Two of the XTs control video routing switchers. One of them directs automatic playback of videotapes through a CCTV network to a motel complex that houses students enrolled in Aetna's training program. Most of this activity takes place in the evenings; thus, the computer control cuts down on personnel.

The company also managed the development of teleconferencing scheduling/control software that allows the department to automatically control, via a Utah Scientific router, the switching and management of a national teleconferencing network. (Aetna and IBM jointly own Satellite Business Systems, which operates 12 teleconferencing rooms in Hartford, CT; Chicago, IL; McLean, VA; and Walnut Creek, CA.) In addition to controlling the switching activities between the sites, the micro tracks and stores information concerning numbers of bookings, names of clients, billing, and uplink and downlink arrangement. It also generates work orders. According to Richard O'Keefe, department head, the micro is invaluable in the teleconferencing operation, because it not only controls the system on a daily basis, but can provide an overall status report alerting the staff to potential problems.

O'Keefe reports that his department's micro experience has proven to be "better than I had expected." He cautions those about to purchase a micro to choose the operating system that is most versatile and that is unlikely to be discontinued or abandoned by the vendor.

BUICK MOTOR DIVISION
Flint, MI

Subsidiary of: General Motors Corp.
Type of facility: In-house corporate studio
Population served: Employees
Micro owned: IBM PC
Software packages owned: Lotus 1-2-3, WordStar, dBase III
Contact: David Collins

An IBM PC was acquired by the Buick video department two years ago, when video communications manager David Collins asked management for some clerical assistance. "Instead of giving me a person, they gave me a machine," he comments. But the hardware is working well for Collins and his six-person staff, who produce some 65 videotapes of varying lengths annually.

Collins' department operates on total chargeback, which requires "excellent bookkeeping," according to the manager. He uses Lotus 1-2-3 to balance the books monthly and finds that doing so not only saves a good deal of time, but also increases accuracy. Hardware repair and maintenance records are also tracked on the PC.

The WordStar word-processing program is used for scriptwriting, which Collins says is a lifesaver when it is time to make the inevitable revisions. The program is also used to generate teleprompter copy that is fed through the department's Q-TV system. According to the Buick manager, this setup expedites the entire scriptwriting/teleprompting process.

Another task for which the department has found the PC invaluable involves communications relating to the daily internal cable television program it produces. The clips feature Buick staffers, all of whom must be contacted by the department to arrange for taping, and most of whom have never appeared on camera. Before acquiring the PC, the video department had to write individually to each person scheduled to be profiled. Now, the information—such as what to wear, where to report for taping and how to act in front of the camera—is in the computer, and when necessary, the department runs a one-page memo with specific requirements for a particular person. This "greatly increases our efficiency in preparing for these programs," says Collins.

The PC has also helped the department handle routine written communications with people outside the organization. Letters to students seeking internships, job applicants and the like are stored and customized as needed.

But the microcomputer accomplishment of which Collins is most proud took 18 months to carry out and has only recently been completed. Using dBase III, his staff members organized and categorized every production the department has produced since 1979, and they recently published a catalog that includes more than 600 entries. This marks the first time since 1983 that the department has issued a catalog, and this year's entry is far more complete than its predecessor.

Also using dBase III, the department has filed alphabetically, by subject and by title, the daily internal cable programs it produces. This enables staffers to search, for instance, for all productions that have the word "Buick" in the title or those that deal with "quality."

Everyone in the Buick video department uses the IBM PC, but Collins says the learning process was at times difficult. "We're trained in video, not computers," he explains. But many of the obstacles have been overcome, and Collins estimates the micro is in use approximately 75% of the working day.

The manager plans to use the PC more for tasks like pre-production, inventory control and maintenance record keeping as time permits. As for disappointments, Collins reports there have been few. "Our major frustration is in trying to adequately master the software," he says.

Collins "strongly" recommends the PC to others. He suggests that those thinking of purchasing a system talk with peers who have micros and fully explore all options before making a decision.

CSIU-TV
Lewisburg, PA

Subsidiary of: Central Susquehanna Intermediate Unit
Type of facility: Cable access
Population served: General public
Micros owned: Apple Macintosh
Software packages owned: MacWrite, MacPaint, Multiplan
Contact: Steve Naugle, coordinator of media services

Budgeting, scriptwriting and correspondence are the most frequent applications for which the Apple Macintosh installed at CSIU-TV is used. The unit is one of 40 located in the 10 departments of the facility's parent, a state education agency.

Steve Naugle, coordinator of media services at the station, had it easier than many of his peers when asking management to approve the micro purchase. Because his is an education agency, "the whole place is computer-oriented," he explains. "I didn't have to convince them of the idea." The micro was acquired in 1984 through the state education bidding process. All units in the system are serviced by an in-house repair shop that also handles software.

Naugle devotes at least half the work week to the micro. Much of this time is spent on budgeting tasks that are accomplished two thirds faster than would be possible manually, he estimates.

The micro enables him to turn out per-production financial plans and cost analyses, which, for a cable access center that serves a population of some 40,000, can be an almost unmanageable task. Program logs are also maintained on the system.

As for production tasks, Naugle uses the Macintosh for teleprompting, as well as for the offline generation of characters and graphics. He considers the micro a "definite timesaver" and expects to purchase additional units.

Naugle warns those about to buy a micro that there are "many different computers available with many differences among them." He stresses the importance of identifying the facility's needs and of taking time in making a selection. "It's an investment in your department's future," he warns.

DELTAK, INC.
Naperville, IL

Subsidiary of: Prentice Hall/Gulf + Western
Type of facility: Video publishing
Population served: Clients
Micros owned: IBM PCs
Software packages owned: Lotus 1-2-3, dBase II, VisiCalc Advanced, ExecuVision
Contact: Michael Janowski, video production scheduler

The television department at Deltak, which produces or acquires some 400 video programs per year for business clients, has two IBM PCs (256K and 512K), purchased in 1983. In peak periods, some of the six PCs installed in the company's information center can be used by the television facility staff (see Figure 3.1).

According to Deltak's Michael Janowski, video production scheduler, more than half of the television department's 20-person staff regularly work on the PCs, which are in use about 75% of the work day. At present, they are used to carry out studio and production management tasks, though Janowski reports that the department is looking for a PC-based graphics system that actually lives up to its impressive specs.

Calling the amount of work turned out on the micros "amazing," Janowski claims that the technology has been of the greatest value in easing the budgeting process. What used to be a painstaking procedure that sometimes took two days to "domino" (work out every possibility with ripple effects throughout the budget), can now be accomplished in just hours. Several "what if" scenarios can be analyzed and appropriately budgeted.

The micros have also made Deltak's television department more competitive in bidding custom jobs for clients. Items can easily be added or deleted, and bids can be manipulated to adapt to a variety of specifications.

Scheduling and inventory control are two other important tasks accomplished with the PCs. Weekly schedules are generated, part-timers' and freelancers' hours are tracked, and the original and edited master tape library and special effects library are

Part III: Profiles 53

Figure 3.1: Deltak, Inc.'s television facility staff uses IBM PCs.

logged. Personnel records and production statistics are being put into the system, and Janowski is planning generate quarterly schedules.

Janowski cautions that those new to micros must be prepared to experience downtime as staffers learn to use the technology. Though the Deltak television department employees are probably more computer literate than average (the nature of the company's business is data processing), he says there were some problems at the beginning because "management didn't think we needed time to get used to the micros."

To those about to choose a micro, Janowski says, "Shop around. You don't have to get a PC. Make a small investment first, and then if you need more power, get more."

GENERAL FOODS
White Plains, NY

Type of facility: In-house corporate studio
Population served: Employees
Micro owned: IBM PC
Software packages owned: Lotus 1-2-3, The Bottom Line, DataEase
Contact: Bill Hoppe, manager

The General Foods Video Center—which turns out some 50 programs annually for the company's 60,000 employees—purchased an IBM PC in 1985 to assist with "housekeeping" tasks, according to Bill Hoppe, manager of the facility. The move turned out to be a wise one: most of the department's five-member staff as well as the freelancers who are frequently employed use the micro. Hoppe estimates that the micro is in service between two and three hours per day.

To draft production budgets, the General Foods facility uses Marc Bauman's The Bottom Line (see the Lincoln Center for the Performing Arts profile in this section). Hoppe says that before the purchase of the PC, budgeting was the department's most time-consuming task. (The facility charges for out-of-pocket expenses plus override.) Now, accurate and professional-looking budgets can be worked out in one third of the time—and with far less stress, adds the manager.

Hoppe finds The Bottom Line a timesaver not only in doing the actual budgeting, but in presenting the budget information to the client. The department uses a "project summary sheet" included in the software and adapted for the General Foods facility to issue production cost estimates. The client sees this summary of the budget but never sees the actual budget.

While the budget contains numerous line items and columns to enable the video department to appropriate dollars for every facet of production, the client's summary letter contains only five categories that correspond to line items in the budget. These are pre-production, production, post-production, distribution and video center charges. A total budget figure is also given. Hoppe explains that the PC is working so well because it enables the department to create precise and detailed budgets while allowing the simple generation of this client form containing only the most important figures. The result, according to Hoppe, is a budget presentation that is simple for the client to understand but also has a professional appearance.

Hoppe is especially proud of a project the department just completed with the help of the micro and Liza Sullivan, a freelance producer who is also "at home" on the PC. Using DataEase, a template used in conjunction with Lotus, the facility has published a catalog (see Figure 3.2) of the General Foods video library that has been distributed throughout the company. It gives program name, running time, date of production and other relevant information for some 200 titles available from the department. The data were transferred via telephone modem to another building, where the General Foods print shop is located. "We were never able to issue a complete catalog before," explains Hoppe. "This will be a big help to the managers we serve, as well as to our department."

DataEase has also been used to create a "facilities request form" that producers fill out for each project on which they are working. It includes information on the people involved in the shoot and how to reach them, the facilities and equipment needed for each particular day and other details. This has helped the department to be more organized and efficient, says Hoppe, who notes that the ease with which changes can be made acts as an incentive to those using the system.

Encouraged by the success of the program catalog, Hoppe hopes soon to create a catalog of slides and stock footage to reduce the time it takes to locate and retrieve particular items. The PC would also be used to keep a "vendors' book" of goods and services, had this not been developed on the department's Wang before the purchase of the micro.

Hoppe would like to be able to use the IBM for list management. The department has a cuts-only offline edit system for window dubs. Currently, the numbers must be manually typed into the editor, and Hoppe hopes eventually to interface the two pieces of hardware to eliminate this task.

In all, the General Foods facility's experience with the IBM PC has been positive. Hoppe advises other managers to purchase a micro "to get training and experience if nothing else." He says

Part III: Profiles 57

MANUFACTURING OPERATIONS
VIDEO CENTER

NEW SYSTEMS & TECHNOLOGY

CIM — COMPUTER INTEGRATED MANUFACTURING Code #: 0128A
1985 Operators Conference

CIM authorities Dr. John Goldhar of the Illinois Institute, Tom Gunn from Arthur D. Little Co., and G.F.(Buck) Rogers, consultant, discuss the key advantages, benefits and implications CIM will have on General Foods manufacturing. (Produced: May 1985, Length: 35 minutes)

CIM — COMPUTER INTEGRATED MANUFACTURING Code #: 0128B
"A Key to Competitive Superiority"

Harvey Walzer, Director of Corporate Quality Assurance at General Foods, introduces CIM authorities Dr. John Goldhar, Dean of the Illinois Institute; Tom Gunn, V.P. Arthur D. Little Co.; and G.F. (Buck) Rogers, Consultant. They discuss the key advantages, benefits and implications CIM will have on GF operations. (Produced: May 1985, Length: 39 minutes)

Note: Same as above program (Code # 0128a) but contains an introduction by Harvey Walzer.

ENERGY CONSERVATION I & II Code #: 0005

This program shows two examples of how energy conservation is possible at plant and warehouse facilities. Part I — The Dover Exchanger; Part II — The Lafayette Computer. (Produced: May 1980, Length: 4 minutes)

MANUFACTURING COST MANAGEMENT SYSTEM Code #: 0112

Hal Golle, V.P. — Group Executive, Operations, and Tom Hoeppner, V.P. and Controller, discuss the implementation of the MCM System in all General Foods plants. Program also provides an overview of how the system works. (Produced: April 1985, Length: 13 minutes)

QUALITY ASSURANCE

QUALITY TECHNOLOGY IN OPERATIONS Code #: 0064
"The Productivity Link"

A three-part program on the subject of productivity at General Foods. 1) Vice President Hal Golle discusses the manufacturing vision. 2) Dr. J.S. Hunter of Princeton University stresses the importance of modern statistics in operations. 3) Phil Smith comments to underscore the importance of productivity to General Foods. (Produced: April 1984, Length: 38 minutes)

— 27 —

Figure 3.2: Sample page of General Foods' 1986 Video Program Catalog.

that the production people will find the micro most useful in budgeting and production control. The manager cautions, however, that learning to use a micro takes a good deal of time, and the department that happens to have a computer whiz in its midst is lucky. At the General Foods facility, this person is the chief engineer, who, according to Hoppe, has been "extremely valuable" in helping the staffers learn their way around the micro. "All the manuals, books and articles in the world are not nearly as valuable as having someone nearby who knows it," he adds.

HAWAIIAN ELECTRIC CO.
Honolulu, HI

Type of facility: In-house corporate studio
Population served: General public, employees, stockholders
Micros owned: Apple II, IBM PC
Software packages owned: Apple Writer III, Apple Graphics, WordStar, Displaywriter
Contact: Scott Shirai, audiovisual specialist

A one-man shop limited by budget constraints, the Hawaiian Electric video department purchased a 128K Apple II in 1982 and a 256K IBM PC in 1984. Audiovisual specialist Scott Shirai spends about 20% of his time on the computers; the Apple gets the most use.

Shirai finds the technology invaluable for such studio management tasks as correspondence; budgeting; scheduling; inventory control; and cataloging and filing the media library, music/sound effects and stock footage. He also generates scripts on the computers, but the Apple was originally bought for production purposes.

Shirai says that combining the Apple with the Chyron VP-1 character generator and graphics software has "worked out extremely well," considering the budgetary constraints he faced when buying the system. He purchased the computers from a computer dealer and the VP-1 from his video dealer. Like many in the industry, Shirai found little support from the computer vendor; it was his video dealer who provided the most technical assistance.

Teamed with the VP-1, the Apple creates low-end graphics, including titles, pie charts and bar graphs. Shirai calls the graphics quality "adequate," but hopes to enhance the output later this year by interfacing the IBM PC with the video system.

In 1982 it was difficult to find NTSC-compatible PCs, says Shirai, who, because of the wide selection now available, envies those about to make a purchase. If he were starting anew, he would buy an IBM AT and a complete software package that would enable him to do animation. Shirai estimates that the software would run about $10,000, a price that he deems small, considering the increased quality and flexibility.

HOBART CORP.
Troy, OH

Type of facility: In-house corporate studio
Population served: Employees, customers
Micros owned: IBM AT, IBM Displaywriter, Atari 800
Software packages owned: Lotus 1-2-3, dBase III, Displaywrite 2, Reportpack, Textpack
Contact: Paul Hinkelman, manager of audiovisual services

Hobart Audiovisual Services produces approximately 35 programs per year to meet the employee training and customer support needs of the world's largest producer of commercial food preparation and cleanup equipment. The IBM AT, purchased in 1985, is the most recent acquisition; the Atari 800 was bought in 1983 and the IBM Displaywriter was acquired in 1982.

The AT is used primarily in studio and production management (see Figure 3.3). Scripts are created on the micro to simplify the revision process, and the end product feeds a continuous-run teleprompter used in Hobart's studio. The script is run on computer-type endless paper that works with the teleprompter system. The staff must paginate the script again to delete spaces that would otherwise appear between pages. Using the micro for scriptwriting, according to Paul Hinkelman, manager of audiovisual services, has saved the department a great deal of time and effort.

Hinkelman, the primary user of the AT, considers himself a "strong believer in keeping detailed and accurate records, whether or not they are used on a daily basis." Therefore, he also uses the system to keep track of all information concerning internal dedication of resources, outside expenses, time allocations and audiovisual programs. Some of the reports he generates are used internally to keep tabs on budgets; others are given to clients to itemize the expenditures made and internal resources spent. "Because we operate on an out-of-pocket chargeback system," says Hinkelman, "it's important that we're able to tell clients the real value of the service we provide."

All six staff members in the department use the AT, primarily for word processing applications, including correspondence, inventory, label-making and cataloging. In fact, because the AT

Part III: Profiles 61

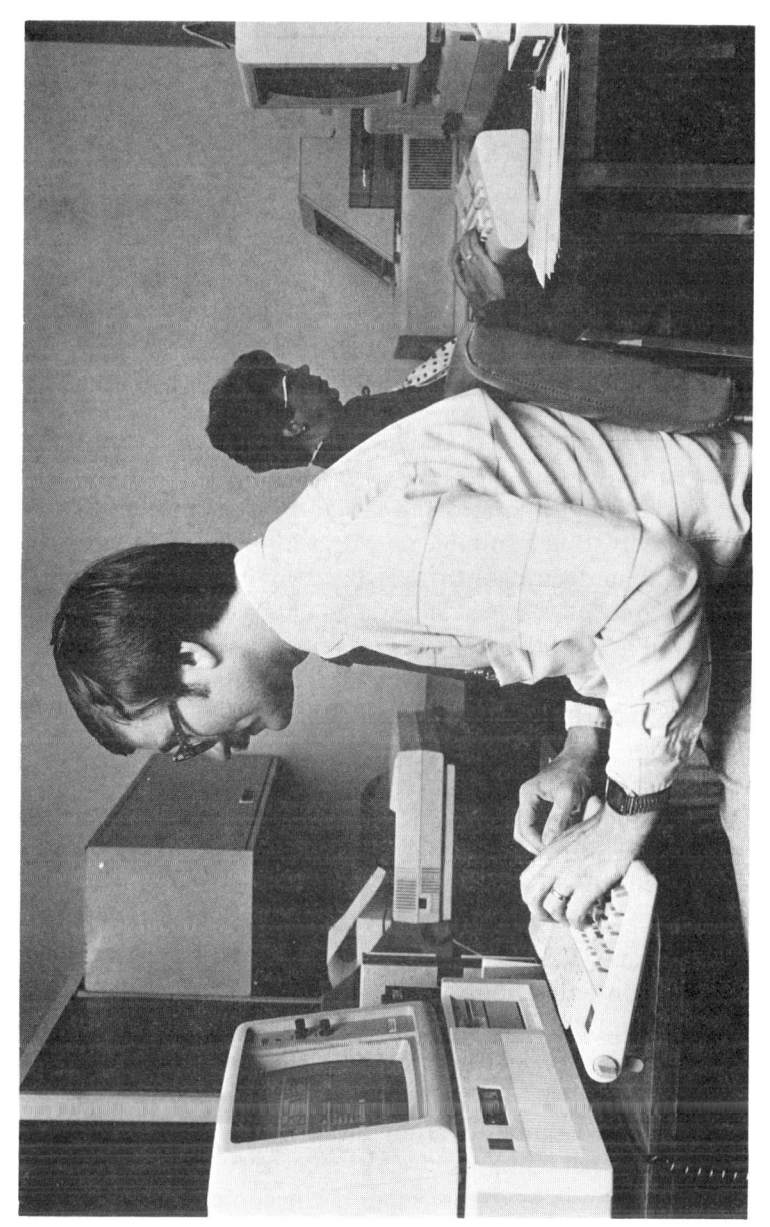

Figure 3.3: Hobart Audiovisual Services staff members use microcomputers for studio and production management.

accepts such a wide variety of software and is so easy to use, the department is considering giving up the Displaywriter, which is essentially only a word processor.

Hinkelman thinks of the micro not as a timesaver, but as a tool that allows his staff to accomplish more than would otherwise be possible. As he explains, upper management was quite skeptical at the outset but is now fully supportive of his venture into the computer age.

> There was a view that a micro is like a typewriter, and there was some sensitivity about a middle manager such as myself sitting down and working out programs and systems for hours at a time. Now that they see the end result—the sophistication of the data we can generate—there are no problems.

The Atari 800 is tied into the department's production equipment. Currently interfaced with a switcher and editor, it controls some record-keeping functions and generates shot logs. Hinkelman is working on creating a suitable edit decision list (EDL) as well as on automating hardware control via the switcher and micro. "It's a wonderful concept that a computer costing a couple of hundred dollars can run a $15,000 switcher," he muses.

But progress is not as smooth as Hinkelman would like or thinks is possible. He sees great potential in interfacing production equipment with micros, and he would ultimately like to have one computer in the control room for more sophisticated EDL management, information storage and retrieval, and effects and character generator control. "In theory, I'll be able to interconnect it all at some point and have one source of information and control in the studio," he explains.

The Hobart AV manager also reports that manufacturers make production equipment as simple as they can or as complex as they have to. But the internal capabilities of the machines extend a little beyond that and can be challenged by a micro. The difficulty lies in getting vendor support. "The manufacturers can do a better job of helping us. They all love the concept of pairing production equipment and micros, but offer very little assistance," he says. In Hinkelman's experience, only the equipment designers—

not the salespeople or customer service reps—know the actual capabilities of the hardware, but they do not consider helping users such as himself a high priority. "More people have to bug the manufacturers for this kind of information," he adds.

Overall, the move to micros was an extremely positive one for the Hobart department. Hinkelman advises others about to purchase a system not to buy just a word processor, because the software programs made for personal computers are much more sophisticated and flexible. In addition, he thinks that the first software purchases should include a word processing program and a database program for records management.

IMC INSTRUCTIONAL TELEVISION CENTER
Boston, MA

Subsidiary of: Suffolk University
Type of facility: In-house studio
Population served: Faculty, staff, students
Micros owned: Apple IIe
Software packages owned: Screen Writer, DB Master
Contact: Bill Walcott, instructional television coordinator

Bill Walcott, instructional television coordinator, says the Apple IIe, purchased a few years ago, has been great help in managing filing and budgeting tasks, as well as in script generation. Record-keeping and report generation tasks done on the micro have proven "very successful," and studio catalogs and files—including the media library—have been logged. The IIe has also been valuable in scriptwriting; Walcott says he has had no problems with the one-column output.

One of the keys to maximizing a system's usefulness, advises Walcott, is to show as many people as possible how to use it. "Don't keep it in the exclusive preserve of one person." He continues, "We've found that the more people familiar with the system, the better." The five-person staff at the IMC Instructional Television Center—plus a number of work-study students—puts in a total of some 10 hours per week on the IIe.

Nevertheless, Walcott says that the IIe is slow and that the software available is very limiting. He also reports that the IIe's 64K memory is just not sufficient for his operation.

Eventually, Walcott would like to be able to control VCR playback with a micro, be it the IIe or another unit purchased in the future. He adds that if he were buying a micro for the first time now, he would opt for the Macintosh.

JOHN STANLEY TRAINING PROGRAMS
Los Gatos, CA

Type of facility: Video publishing
Population served: Clients
Micros owned: Apple IIe
Software packages owned: Appleworks, Graphics Department, 4 in One
Contact: John Stanley, director

This producer of video training programs, also known as The Information Factory, purchased its Apple IIe with monitor, duo disk drive and extended 80-column card in 1984. Director John Stanley has had much success with the system.

Stanley says the micro has been a big timesaver, reducing his workload by at least 10%. And at his rather substantial per-hour rate, that's a significant accomplishment, he points out. The company produces more than 30 programs annually, primarily for industrial clients. Four of the staffers use the computer regularly.

The four applications for which the IIe is used most heavily include word processing, mail merge, simple accounting and teleprompting. His graphics package is used to generate art that is included in the student manuals often accompanying the videotapes.

Stanley contends that word processing is "so far beyond beating yourself to death on a typewriter." Correspondence and other paperwork management tasks—including financial analyses, personnel record keeping and inventory control—have been highly productive on the IIe. A mail merge program is used to respond to postcard mailers produced by the firm, and accounts receivable, accounts payable and billing are tracked with the micro.

But perhaps the most innovative use of the IIe at the firm entails teleprompting. Stanley has devised a system by which the script is entered on the micro, margins are set and the script is run on 3-inch-wide adding machine tape. The paper is then pulled through a holding jig under a video camera and recorded on videotape. (Reverse polarity results in white letters on a black background.) There are 25 1/2-inch-wide characters per line. Fast and slow tape speeds allow the talent to choose the more comfortable rate. Stanley plans to market the teleprompter program (for the

IIe and IIc) on a disk that provides "plenty of space" for the script and that can be copied onto additional disks, as required by script length.

Like Bill Walcott of the IMC Instructional Television Center (see preceding case study), Stanley would choose the Apple Macintosh if purchasing today. As for others interested in buying a computer, Stanley warns, "Double your initial estimate as to how long it will take you to proficiently operate the software!"

KFYR-TV
Bismarck, ND

Subsidiary of: Meyer Broadcasting
Type of facility: Broadcast studio
Population served: General public
Micros owned: IBM PCs, IBM XTs
Software packages owned: dBase III, Lotus 1-2-3, Multiplan, MultiMate, PC FILE III
Contact: Don Bachmeier, production

The parent company of this NBC affiliate, strongly supportive of the use of personal computers for both corporate and personal work, finances the purchase of IBM PCs interest-free for two years to encourage employees to investigate their uses. The machines are so popular that some of the employees have bought them to keep at work to ensure ready accessibility. The company makes evaluation copies of many popular software packages available to the employees, and the employee newsletter regularly carries microcomputer information to keep users aware of new developments.

Don Bachmeier's production department acquired its first computer in 1983 and has been adding them since then; a number are owned by the staff. About half the department's 10 staff members use the micros. Standard operations include word processing, budgeting and filing. Everything from raw tape footage logs to personnel records are maintained on the micros and the department has developed its own software to track personnel expenses. The engineering department makes frequent use of the technology's number-crunching abilities.

As for production tasks, the department is just dabbling in IBM-assisted graphics with the Chyron IV. But because it is involved in such a visually oriented business, the station tries to keep abreast of developments in the microcomputer/graphics arena.

Bachmeier is certain that the micros have made his department more efficient and accurate. He advises those interested in purchasing a computer to "do it now!" But he cautions those about to do so to "know what you want it for, be sure you need it, buy all the memory you can afford and talk to someone who has done it."

LAND O' LAKES
Minneapolis, MN

Type of facility: In-house corporate studio
Population served: Employees
Micros owned: IBM PC, Apple Macintosh, Magi
Software packages owned: Symphony, Titlewriter, Dicomed Presenter, MacWrite, MacPaint, Microsoft Chart
Contact: Dennis Karlstad, manager

The IBM PC, Macintosh and Magi are used for a great number and variety of tasks at Land O' Lakes' three-member department of Electronic Media Services. First on board was the Magi (1983), followed by the IBM PC (1984) and then the Apple Macintosh (1985).

Though the Magi is still used to produce graphics and slides, the IBM PC is connected to a Chyron VP-1 character generator and is the primary workhorse of the department. A color jet printer was recently added to the setup, as were a color graphics board and color monitor. The newly acquired Dicomed Presenter software enables the IBM to produce slides.

In addition, the micro is used for studio and production management tasks, including scriptwriting, inventorying, budgeting and billing. Says manager Dennis Karlstad, "It's delightful. We're even printing out our storyboards!"

The Macintosh is used primarily as a word processing tool and as a graphics generator. Karlstad reports that virtually no staff time was lost in learning the Macintosh and that the micro was "almost instantly productive." The PC, on the other hand, was more difficult to learn. But the downtime was lessened considerably because the company maintains a computer users' center where employees are given an opportunity to explore the technology hands-on.

The Land O' Lakes manager is delighted with the efficiency and flexibility afforded by the micros. His ideal—though it will probably never be realized—is to be able to generate his scripts, storyboards and slides from one terminal, which would also act as an edit controller. It would be wonderful, too, he adds, if the terminal were also connected to a disk player that had the company's 50,000 historical slides ready for access.

Karlstad has found computer dealers to be less than helpful. "They sell you what they want to sell you and really don't care," he comments. He advises first-time buyers to shop around and not to be intimidated into purchasing everything from one dealer.

LEXCOM PRODUCTIONS
West Columbia, SC

Type of facility: Production
Population served: Clients
Micros owned: Sony SMC-70G
Software packages owned: SuperCalc, Letter Writer, Mail List, Record Management, CPM Operating System
Contact: Dale Thomas, manager

The Sony SMC-70G, purchased in 1983, is not working out as well as expected for LexCom Productions, according to manager Dale Thomas. The unit, chosen by the production company because few systems available at the time performed both graphics and personal computer functions, has proven to be limited by a lack of software and too slow.

Though its performance as a studio management aid—in budgeting, word processing and the like—is acceptable, the 70G falls short as a production tool, says Thomas. Purchased primarily for its graphics capabilities, the 70G drives a Chyron VP-1 character generator. But the operation is "terribly slow," according to Thomas, who finds the CPM-based system cumbersome and tedious to work with.

LexCom had originally purchased a Sony SMC-70, then upgraded to the 70G because of its ability to superimpose on video. But the output "looks too digitized," says Thomas, who adds that he is "unhappy with the graphics, given the options available with today's technology."

When it comes time to replace the computer, Thomas believes LexCom will select an IBM PC and a Chyron VP-2 character generator. As he says, "The SMC-70G has its place in a small shop, but it's just not for us."

Thomas advises those about to purchase a microcomputer to choose a system that is IBM-compatible. He also cautions against taking what seems like the easy way out—that is, buying a system that can act both as a graphics generator and as a personal computer. "I've learned that a computer can't be all things to all people in a facility," says Thomas, who explains that having secretaries and production people vie for time on the SMC-70G "just doesn't work."

LINCOLN CENTER FOR THE PERFORMING ARTS
New York, NY

Type of facility: Broadcast (provides live broadcasts from Lincoln Center)
Population served: General public
Micros owned: Wang PCs
Software packages owned: Lotus 1-2-3, dBase II, Wang Word Processing and several templates designed by the user
Contact: Marc Bauman, department head

Lincoln Center for the Performing Arts has 20 Wang PCs in all; two of them are located in the production department headed by Marc Bauman. The 256K Wangs were purchased in 1984, and Bauman wonders how he ever did his job before getting the computers.

The Wangs are used for a host of studio and production management tasks, including correspondence, scheduling, inventorying, cataloging, budgeting and script generation. But it is with specially designed templates that Bauman has been able to fully explore the capabilities of micros within the television industry.

Through his own company, The Bottom Line (Pelham, NY), Bauman is marketing a series of computer templates driven by Lotus 1-2-3 and usable on IBM, Wang, Texas Instruments, DEC Rainbow and Compaq computers. To date, there are six available: Production Cost Estimate Template, Shotsheet Template, Production Scheduling Template, Payroll Template, Timing Template and Paper Edit Template. A package consisting of the first four sells for $750; the two remaining are $150 each.

The Production Cost Estimate Template enables the user to budget and track 243 different line items, ranging from animals to wardrobe. It computes estimated costs, actual costs and variables, and it can recalculate an entire budget in nine seconds, says Bauman. The Shotsheet Template assigns and sorts camera shots; Bauman himself uses it in taping "Live at Lincoln Center," which is a nine-camera production. The Production Scheduling Template is used to organize a production schedule based on a shooting script. Scenes, actors or locations can be sorted in different combinations to produce an efficient shooting schedule.

The Payroll Template is used to provide estimates on crew costs or detailed crew actuals, including salary, penalties and benefits. The Timing Template is used to calculate cumulative running time based on individual segment lengths. And the Paper Edit Template is designed to aid in offline editing. The user inputs the segment number, segment title, reel number and transition type. Then, using SMPTE time code, the user enters the edit in and edit out points. The computer calculates each segment length and cumulative, or record out, length. This template can also use the Lotus 1-2-3 sort capabilities to rearrange an edit list for the greatest flexibility.

Bauman says the micro has changed his sense of time. "If it now takes me six minutes to do something that used to take me 60, I'm frustrated because it didn't take five minutes," adding that he could never go back to doing the various tasks by hand.

Bauman cautions, however, that a computer is not a solution to sloppy management. He warns that good organizational skills are crucial to preparing to use a computer. Noting that the learning process can be a slow one, Bauman likens learning to use a computer to learning a new language. But he hastens to add that "it's very clear to me that you can't be competitive in this business if you don't have the speed that computers afford."

MERCK & CO., INC.
Rahway, NJ

Type of facility: In-house corporate studio
Population served: Employees
Micro owned: IBM PC
Software packages owned: Lotus 1-2-3, The Leading Edge, Associate Producer, Cross Talk, DataFax
Contact: Jeffrey Goldstein, manager, corporate audiovisual services

The public affairs department of this major pharmaceutical manufacturer acquired an IBM PC in 1984, according to Jeffrey Goldstein, manager of corporate audiovisual services. Wang predominates at Merck; the IBM was purchased when the department was involved in evaluating the merits of establishing a videotex system for the company. The idea has since been dropped; Goldstein concludes that "videotex is a solution looking for a problem." Other uses for the microcomputer have since been found, and a hard card was recently added so that programs could be stored, thereby reducing software-loading time.

Lotus 1-2-3 and the Leading Edge are the two programs most often used by the department, which relies heavily upon freelancers and turns out some 15 videotapes annually. Goldstein uses Lotus—which he has adapted for his own needs—to draft production budgets that are "neater, easier to do and more up-to-date" than were the budgets presented in longhand before the PC's arrival. The AV manager enjoys the freedom afforded by the micro's ability to "ripple" the effects of a change throughout an entire budget, and he says the technology allows him to keep a more watchful eye on the budgets of productions in progress.

For word processing, the department uses The Leading Edge. Goldstein, who says he was a good typist before getting the PC, writes most of his own letters, memos and reports on the IBM. "Because I dictate less, my secretary is free to do other things, which makes the department more productive on the whole," adds the manager. He estimates that he spends about one hour per day at the micro.

The IBM is also used for teleprompting in field productions. The scripts are input and then printed out on a paper roll for use by on-camera talent.

Cross Talk is used for computer conferencing. Through Compu-Serve, Goldstein, who is cochair of a computer users' group, is able to communicate with others nationwide.

Goldstein, who admits to "going bananas ordering software" after getting the micro, made two purchases—The Associate Producer and DataFax—that turned out to be mistakes for the Merck department. Goldstein found that the former, a budgeting program, incorporates line items and category breakdowns that seem geared toward independent producers rather than in-house departments. He adds that while The Associate Producer is simpler to learn than is Lotus, it is also less flexible.

The second software mistake was DataFax, which Goldstein initially purchased to catalog the department's stock footage. Although a student intern input all of the data, Goldstein soon found that the program was not only difficult to learn, but was relatively ineffective as a search tool because of its inability to search by keyword combinations. The data has been transferred to the department's Wang, which offers powerful search capabilities.

While he considers the micro invaluable, Goldstein advises others to evaluate software purchases carefully and to be realistic in estimating how much time it will take to learn to operate the hardware.

Goldstein also cautions that "first-time computer users have to be prepared to go through an uncomfortable learning period." He points out that once out of school, most adults spend time perfecting a craft, but few take on the task of learning a new skill. "This can lead to computer phobia," he warns. "You're suddenly in an area which makes you feel inept, stupid and uncomfortable. But almost everyone has gone through it and made the same mistakes." Is it worth the trouble? Definitely, according to the Merck manager. "A computer can really help you in your work. Besides, it's fun!"

OKLAHOMA POLICE DEPARTMENT TRAINING CENTER
Oklahoma City, OK

Type of facility: In-house corporate studio
Population served: Police and fire department employees
Micros owned: Apple IIe
Software packages owned: Apple Writer, PFS: FILE
Contact: Dale Bruns, audiovisual production specialist

The 64K Apple IIe purchased by the television department in 1984 is one of four housed at the Police Department Training Center. (Others are used to track classes and the like.)

According to audiovisual production specialist Dale Bruns, the computer was purchased to drive a Chyron VP-1 character generator. This remains its primary function. Though the setup runs "a little slower" than he would like, Bruns says he is more than satisfied with the quality of the generated material and the ease with which the system can be accessed.

Since it is just beginning to explore the many other options afforded by the micro, the facility does not yet have a printer. But because the department turns out some seven programs per month for fire and police personnel, Bruns has found the Apple IIe invaluable in cataloging finished videotapes and inventorying hardware and blank tapes. The PFS: FILE program is used for these purposes.

Bruns expects to add peripherals and increase his computer software library in the future. He advises those about to select a micro to "be sure to see demonstrations of a variety of computers so you can tell which are most adaptable to your needs." For those loath to spend money on a computer because they are working on a tight budget, Bruns adds, "A micro's versatility is its primary selling point for a facility with a limited budget."

P. A. BERGNER & CO.
Peoria, IL

Type of facility: In-house corporate studio
Population served: Employees
Micros owned: TRS-80 Model II
Software packages owned: VisiCalc, Scripsit, Multiplan
Contact: John Teegarden, video producer

The 64K TRS-80 Model II on board at the headquarters of this 25-store retail chain will be in use "until it dies," according to video producer John Teegarden. Acquired in 1982, the Radio Shack unit is used primarily as a word processor. It generates all typewritten materials (correspondence, labels, budgets, etc.) put out by the department, and it is used some eight hours per week.

But it is for scriptwriting that Teegarden finds the computer invaluable. "My experience has been thrilling when scriptwriting," he comments. "Revisions can be made, printed and returned before anyone has time to forget the reasons for the revisions. This cuts down on third- and fourth-guessing."

Teegarden hopes to buy an NTSC-adaptable system eventually, and he advises those about to purchase a computer to do the same. He says the ability to create even rudimentary graphics would be an immeasurable saver of both time and money.

THE PRUDENTIAL
Newark, NJ

Type of facility: In-house corporate studio
Population served: Employees
Micros owned: IBM AT, IBM XT, IBM PC, Compaq, Compaq Plus, Amqute, 2 Leading Edges
Software packages owned: Lotus 1-2-3, DataEase, MultiMate, R:Base 5000, Dicomed PC Presenter
Contact: Richard E. Van Deusen, manager

The Audio Visual Communications Division of The Prudential acquired its first micro—the IBM PC—in 1983, and has purchased additional compatible units of various makes and models since. About half of the department's 25-person staff uses the micros, and manager Richard E. Van Deusen readily admits, "I don't know how on earth we ever managed before we got the computers."

Because of the compatibility of the hardware, many of the tasks are carried out on a variety of the micros. Among the applications developed by this division are preparation and revision of legal contracts with suppliers and joint venture partners, preparation and formatting of scripts for teleprompting, revision of letters of agreement with directors and writers, development and production of facility rental marketing letters, maintenance of company-wide audiovisual staff listings, facility schedules and project listings, development of major project proposals and reports, and drafting of production budget estimates and facility rental estimates and invoices.

The department also uses the micros to produce regular and specialized accounting reports, mailing list address labels of clients, and freelance crew payment invoices and vouchers; update and maintain a chargeback system and audiovisual equipment inventory; access company-wide computer-based communications networks; maintain a master videotape catalog and accounting and inventory records for outside joint venture marketing activities; and program multi-image presentations.

For budget estimating, the department had originally purchased VisiCalc. But when Van Deusen found that the software did not meet his department's needs, the switch was made to Lotus, which the manager says has afforded them "a lot more control and accuracy" in many facets of the budgeting process. He adds that most completed productions now finish within 5% of budget. Before the micros were used, "We were lucky if we came within 20%," reports Van Deusen. The budget estimating procedure is part of a Lotus-based "project management system" used by the audiovisual department; the system also includes the project number, production schedule and external facility rental estimate (see Figures 3.4 and 3.5).

Figure 3.4 is a sample of a Lotus database that contains all of the audiovisual department's rates. First, a number of days or units are entered in the column, along with dates. Then the entries are selected and transferred to the schedule of services (see Figure 3.5) section of the worksheet and sorted by date order. The calculations concerning total costs, discounts and taxes are made automatically. The entries for client and project data are entered when the worksheet is first accessed; another computer prints the schedule and saves the data in a file labeled with the project number.

The department uses the AT (equipped with a digital pad for enhanced graphics) for slide graphics and Dicomed PC Presenter software to supply a Genagraphix system. The XT's specialty is its ability to track external business (such as the sale of videotapes) via the R:Base program. The Compaqs were selected for their portability and the Leading Edges for their lower-than-AT price tags. Van Deusen says that while the keyboards may differ somewhat, he and his staff have gotten used to switching back and forth between the various models.

Among the applications now under development are direct communications with regional audiovisual units, a catalog for the department's photographic negative file, preparation and production of equipment shipping invoices and insurance coverage reports; and development of a computer-assisted design program to do set and light plots.

According to Van Deusen, the following are features that video managers should look for when purchasing word-processing and scriptwriting programs.

Part III: Profiles 79

ITEM	UNIT	RATE	NO.	EXTENSION	DATES
Set Build/Light	Day	$700.00	1	$700.00	1 - 2
Set Build/Light	Half-Day	$400.00		$0.00	-
Set Build/Light	Hour O/T	$100.00		$0.00	-
Studio Prod. 1"	Day	$1,200.00	1	$1,200.00	3 -
Studio Prod. 1"	Half-Day	$700.00		$0.00	-
Studio Prod. 1"	Hour O/T	$200.00		$0.00	-
Studio Prod. 3/4"	Day	$1,000.00		$0.00	-
Studio Prod. 3/4"	Half-Day	$600.00		$0.00	-
Studio Prod. 3/4"	Hour O/T	$150.00		$0.00	-
Add'l Camera	Day	$500.00	1	$500.00	3 -
Add'l Camera	Half-Day	$275.00		$0.00	-
Add'l Camera	Hour O/T	$75.00		$0.00	-
Add'l VTR 1"	Day	$500.00		$0.00	-
Add'l VTR 1"	Half-Day	$275.00		$0.00	-
Add'l VTR 1"	Hour O/T	$75.00		$0.00	-
Add'l VTR 3/4"	Day	$150.00		$0.00	-
Add'l VTR 3/4"	Half-Day	$75.00		$0.00	-
Add'l VTR 3/4"	Hour O/T	$25.00		$0.00	-
Prompter 1st	Day	$150.00	1	$150.00	3 -
Prompter 1st	Half-Day	$80.00		$0.00	-
Prompter @ Add'l	Day	$75.00		$0.00	-
Prompter @ Add'l	Half-Day	$40.00		$0.00	-
Wireless Mic. @	Day	$75.00		$0.00	-
Wireless Mic. @	Half-Day	$40.00		$0.00	-
Flats/Set Pieces@	Day	$10.00	5	$50.00	3 -
Carpenters @	Hour	$27.53		$0.00	-
Painters @	Hour	$27.53		$0.00	-
Movers @	Hour	$15.31		$0.00	-
Set Materials	Gross	$0.00		$0.00	-
Studio Crew @	Hour	$45.00		$0.00	-
Studio Crew @	Hour O/T	$60.00		$0.00	-
* AUDIO PRODUCTION				$0.00	-
Audio Studio	Hour	$60.00		$0.00	-
Library Music/FX	Each Use	$5.00		$0.00	-
* REMOTE PRODUCTION				$0.00	-
Remote Prod. 1"	Day	$1,300.00		$0.00	-
Remote Prod. 1"	Half-Day	$800.00		$0.00	-
Remote Prod. 1"	Hour O/T	$200.00		$0.00	-
Remote Prod. 3/4"	Day	$1,100.00		$0.00	-
Remote Prod. 3/4"	Half-Day	$600.00		$0.00	-
Remote Prod. 3/4"	Hour O/T	$175.00		$0.00	-
Add. Cam/Swticher	Day	$500.00		$0.00	-
Add. Cam/Swticher	Half-Day	$300.00		$0.00	-
Add. Cam/Swticher	Hour O/T	$100.00		$0.00	-
Viewfinder Set	Day	$65.00		$0.00	-
Viewfinder Set	Half-Day	$35.00		$0.00	-
Camera Control Un.	Day	$50.00		$0.00	-
Camera Control Un.	Half-Day	$30.00		$0.00	-
Monitor Package	Day	$100.00		$0.00	-
Monitor Package	Half-Day	$60.00		$0.00	-
Prompter System	Day	$150.00		$0.00	-
Prompter System	Half-Day	$80.00		$0.00	-
Baby Legs	Day	$8.00		$0.00	-
Baby Legs	Half-Day	$5.00		$0.00	-
Hi-Hat	Day	$8.00		$0.00	-
Hi-Hat	Half-Day	$5.00		$0.00	-
AC Power Panel	Day	$75.00		$0.00	-
AC Power Panel	Half-Day	$40.00		$0.00	-
Lowell D Kit Add.	Day	$15.00		$0.00	-

Source: The Prudential Insurance Co., 2 Prudential Plaza, Newark, NJ 07101.

Figure 3.4: Sample of a Lotus database featuring Prudential Audio Visual Dept. rates.

```
PRUDENTIAL                          Client: Soap Commercial
AUDIO VISUAL                        Proj. #: 86000
COMMUNICATIONS

                    SCHEDULE OF SERVICES

The following specific services, materials and/or facilities are contracted
to be provided on the dates indicated.

MONTH  DATES       ITEM              UNIT    RATE       NO.  EXTENSION
Aug.   1-2    Set Build/Light        Day     $700.00    1    $700.00
       3-     Studio Prod. 1"        Day     $1,200.00  1    $1,200.00
       3-     Add'l Camera           Day     $500.00    1    $500.00
       3-     Prompter 1st           Day     $150.00    1    $150.00
       3-     Flats/Set Pieces @     Day     $10.00     5    $50.00
       4-     Editing 1", 2 VTR      Hour    $225.00    4    $900.00


Comments: Client to provide tape stock.


Client Name/Address:              SUB-TOTAL . . . . . . . $3,500.00
Art Jones, Creative Director      DISCOUNT . . . . . . . .   $350.00
Super Productions                 NET . . . . . . . . . . . .$3,150.00
700 First Avenue                  SALES TAX @ 6%. . . .    $189.00
Production City, NY 10000                                 ──────────
    Phone #: 212-755-0000         TOTAL ESTIMATE. . .$3,339.00

Purchase Order #:

─────────────────────────────      ─────────────────────────────
For The Prudential                 Client

       Date:      02-Jul-86        Date

By signing this agreement, the lessor agrees to all terms and conditions
as set forth in the standard Terms and Conditions in effect at the time
of signing of this schedule.
```

Source: The Prudential Insurance Co., 2 Prudential Plaza, Newark, NJ 07101.

**Figure 3.5: Sample of a Lotus database featuring
Prudential Audio Visual Dept. schedule of services.**

When buying word-processing programs, managers should keep in mind the guidelines listed below:

- The program must be easy to use. The primary commands must be logical and easy to remember.
- The program should be capable of being loaded on a hard disk and not require a floppy to boot it.
- The "help" menu should be easily accessible.
- The documentation should be well written and easy to understand. Most documentation is written by programmers, who really know more about the program than anyone else needs to know.
- Automatic date stamping in headers or footers to help keep track of revisions, as well as page numbering and repagination, should be available.

When buying scriptwriting programs, managers should check for the following features:

- Two-column and preferably three-column capability if desired, with the ability to toggle back and forth between columns with arrow or function keys.
- Automatic formatting for both two-column and film-style scripts.
- Simultaneous scrolling of both columns and the ability to lift both audio and video together, but also with the ability to deal with them separately as required.
- The ability to print the finished copy in several different styles, including teleprompter format, director's script and script to be sent out with the completed tape.
- Double-spacing and single-spacing available in all columns, user selectable.
- Support of different printers, including daisy wheel, dot matrix and laser jet types.

Van Deusen, who strongly believes that micros can make a good video department even better, warns that the manager of such a department must be willing and able to learn the technology. And, he adds, "Before you go ahead, have a definite application in mind. Unless you have something you really know you want to do, you'll never be able to get started."

RALPHS GROCERY CO.
Compton, CA

Subsidiary of: Federated Department Stores
Type of facility: In-house corporate studio
Population served: Employees
Micros owned: Commodore 64
Software packages owned: PaperClip, The Consultant, Calc Result
Contact: Stephen Brown, television specialist

Unlike the majority of television facilities using microcomputers, the in-house department at Ralphs Grocery owns a Commodore 64 with MSD disk drive. (Only two other companies that responded to the survey use the Commodore, and other departments at Ralphs have IBM PCs).

Stephen Brown, television specialist at Ralphs, knows he broke with tradition by opting for the low-end 64K unit. In fact, he notes that "almost everyone in the video business considers the Commodore a toy." This attitude is compounded by the Commodore's not even being sold in computer specialty stores; it is marketed through retail chains and is frequently heavily discounted.

The purchase was made in 1984 after Brown, who was looking for a computer to interface with the department's VP-1, saw a demonstration of the Commodore running the Chyron character generator at the National Association of Broadcasters convention. Although the Commodore/VP-1 hookup did not have much of a track record, Brown was impressed with the micro's capabilities and its low price. The setup at Ralphs—keyboard, monitor, disk drive and Epson RX-80 printer—totaled just over $1000. Thus far, the department is satisfied with the character and simple graphics generation afforded by the Commodore.

Scriptwriting is another major task for which the micro is used. The three-member television department uses the PaperClip program for this and other word processing applications (correspondence, scheduling, talent records, etc.), and Brown estimates that the computer saves the department 500 to 600 hours annually in scriptwriting time alone.

Brown also finds the Commodore invaluable in drafting budgets and project proposals. Since the Calc Result spreadsheet has been in use, the department has not exceeded budget on any project because "We always know where we stand," explains Brown.

The facility, which provides programs to 130 stores, also inventories its videotapes with the Commodore. This lets the department know, at a glance, where tapes are at any given moment. Information on the wiring in the department's 3/4-inch edit suite is also logged on a disk.

Brown estimates that the micro is in use nearly one quarter of the work day, on average. He lauds the Commodore for its price, flexibility and software availability, but notes that one of its drawbacks is the 40-column display. (Many software programs, such as PaperClip, allow the user to scroll across to 80 columns.)

Being involved in a users' group has been instrumental in helping Brown explore the capabilities of the Commodore, and he advises those in the market for a micro to choose the software first and then find the compatible hardware.

SHADYSIDE HOSPITAL
Pittsburgh, PA

Type of facility: In-house corporate studio
Population served: Employees, patients and general public
Micros owned: Apple IIe
Software packages owned: PFS: FILE, PFS: REPORT, Apple Writer II, Comprehensive PowerScript
Contact: Cyril J. Evans, educational media specialist

Though he wound up with an Apple IIe almost by default—his original request for a Sony SMG-170 was turned down by management—Cyril J. Evans, educational media specialist, has nothing but praise for the micro, acquired in 1984. His is a department of one, augmented by freelancers, and Evans maintains that without the micro, he would be unable to do the job alone. (The IIe was the unit of choice because the hospital was buying a number of micros at the time and was trying to standardize a system.)

The Apple was originally purchased to control a Chyron VP-1 character generator, but its role in the department has expanded to include a variety of studio and production management tasks. Scheduling, budgeting, scriptwriting and inventory control are among the primary applications.

PFS: FILE and PFS: REPORT, says Evans, "give me a new level of control over elements which, with a manual system, caused much grief." The micro gives him instant access to information concerning the whereabouts of hardware and freelancers and permits him to schedule the resources for the coming days. He also maintains sequence logs of all programs produced in-house and has cataloged the department's stock footage and media libraries.

The Apple Writer II program is used for word-processing functions, including correspondence, labeling and shipping. Until the purchase of the Comprehensive PowerScript software, it was also used for scriptwriting, but Evans found the one-column output too inconvenient and cumbersome to work with.

Evans comments that Shadyside's management has been "quite surprised" by the increased level of productivity afforded by the micro. "I have not missed a request for service since getting the Apple," he continues, "and I would not be able to handle the stress of running a one-man show without it."

If he were buying a system today, however, Evans says he would opt for a Chyron VP-2 character generator so that his microcomputer would be freer to perform other functions.

SHOOTER
Aurora, CO

Type of facility: Production
Population served: Clients
Micros owned: Franklin Ace 1000
Software packages owned: Ace Writer, Ace Calc, PFS: FILE, PFS: REPORT, PFS: GRAPH, Personal Financier, Magic Office System, Home Accountant
Contact: J. Michael Russell, owner and producer

"The television production facility not using computers will be left in the dust," maintains J. Michael Russell, owner of Shooter, a broadcast video production company. His 64K Franklin Ace 1000 was purchased in 1984, and is currently outfitted with a modem, two disk drives, 32K print buffer, Speed Demon microprocessor card and Epson printer.

Russell says the unit saves him "countless hours." The producer spends some 10 hours per week on the Franklin, carrying out a host of tasks from budgeting to scriptwriting. Freelancers hired by the producer on a per-project basis are also given access to the Franklin.

Russell believes the technology gives him a real edge over the competition. He cites instances in which he has put together a detailed bid for a client—using all 254 rows of the Ace Calc spreadsheet—in just 30 minutes. And to eliminate the costs of designing and printing business forms, he has generated his own on the computer. They include script forms, music library addition forms, long distance/postage logs, client contact forms, equipment checklists for shoots, client contracts, talent/location releases, maintenance schedules and business mileage logs.

The PFS: FILE program has been used to keep track of the following data: file video (variables are plugged into the computer, which tells what tape(s) the item in question is on); mailing, client and music lists; research; and specialized video.

The computer is also interfaced with a Brother Correctronic typewriter, which has a 1K buffer. This allows information to be input on the Franklin and run through the typewriter.

Though Russell is beginning to outgrow the Franklin's limited memory, he says the computer has freed him to be more creative and to spend more time doing what he's supposed to be doing—producing. Russell hopes to step up to an IBM eventually. He recommends that those in television learn to use computers or consider another line of work.

SPERRY CORP.
Salt Lake City, UT

Type of facility: In-house corporate studio
Population served: Employees of the Communications Software Division
Micros owned: Sperry PCs
Software packages owned: Lotus 1-2-3, PC WRITE, PC FILE, PC CALC, WordStar, dBase, dBase III, PictureIt
Contact: David Spikes, media producer

Sperry's training department (which includes the company's television facility) acquired its PCs between 1983 and 1985. The department's 15 units are part of a company-wide network of some 400 Sperry PCs.

According to media producer David Spikes, the PCs are in use 20 to 30 hours per week, and they cut in half the time spent on such tasks as word processing, scheduling, budgeting and inventory control (see Figure 3.6).

The PCs are also used to design and control interactive tape programs produced by the company.

But it is in the area of graphics that the department has gotten creative. A high-resolution, 10-megabyte PC—paired with the PictureIt software—is used to record graphic images directly onto videotape. Along with the production of word graphics, this combination is used to produce graphics for highlighting and/or boxing items on video. The latter involves the use of a small production switcher (with keying effects) and a frame store unit. Two recent acquisitions that expand the graphics capabilities are a color ink jet printer and a digitizing tablet.

Though Spikes is pleased with the progress made thus far in this area, he is disappointed that graphics generation is so limited at the PC level. He would like to increase the quality and range of the graphics but is being held back by price considerations.

Spikes advises that other facilities planning to install a microcomputer network should be guided by software, not hardware. "Do your homework. First find the software that best suits your needs; then buy the appropriate hardware."

Figure 3.6: Sperry Corp. training department staff members working with Sperry PCs.

VIMART CORP.
Los Gatos, CA

Type of facility: In-house corporate studio
Population served: Clients, employees
Micros owned: Apple IIe, Apple Macintosh, IBM PC, Altos 958
Software packages owned: WordStar, Condor, Multiplan, Microsoft BASIC
Contact: Ric Getter, video manager

ViMart Corp. is a marketing services company specializing in video demonstrations of home computer software. The service features a laserdisc-based kiosk with more than 70 software infomercials on a 60-minute disc.

According to video manager Ric Getter, "Computers are now an essential element" of production. He continues, "They help us perform boring, clerical tasks with tireless perfection, allowing us more time for our creative pursuits." The micros were purchased between 1983 and 1984.

Getter, who is also a successful computer programmer, has developed a set of SMPTE time-code calculators for use in offline edit sessions. First written in Applesoft BASIC, they "greatly improved the speed and accuracy of our time-code and back-timing arithmetic," comments Getter. They were later converted to Microsoft BASIC for use on a variety of computers.

Soon after the company's first prototype laserdisc was produced, it acquired Condor, a simple yet surprisingly powerful (according to Getter) file manager and report writer that is available for a number of micros. This program is used to track the hundreds of software packages that ViMart evaluates for the infomercial discs.

Getter also developed a database to serve as a shot catalog for the firm's master videotapes. Because of the chapter-oriented nature of CLV disks, the department needed to maintain a frame-accurate catalog of each tape. Two databases were integrated to save redundant reentry. The software titles for a disk were "selected" from the inventory database by assigning a production code to each. These were moved, as a group, into the shot catalog database and manually assigned chapter numbers for the laserdisc.

After the edit session, time codes for each chapter were added, taken from the decision list generated by a Mach-1 editing system. Then a BASIC program was run to establish the running times for each chapter, information that was needed for billing purposes. From this, Getter ran a report that was used for chapter-cue insertion. The information also accompanied the disc pre-mastering paperwork sent to 3M in preparation for the mastering and pressing of the laserdisc.

All of the department's scripting and memo writing are done on a word processor. Graphic production designs and storyboards are done on a Macintosh, which Getter calls "a real gem of a PC." The Macintosh, running Microsoft's Multiplan, serves as the studio's accountant. Says the video manager, "It comes as close to fun as any budgeting exercise can."

Getter cautions that his department's great success with micros is due, in part, to the abundance of computer expertise within ViMart. The company's ability to design and write its own software has been invaluable, he says, because the market is just beginning to bring out computer software specifically tailored for the video production industry.

The strongest asset for a studio planning to use micros is a staff member already familiar with both video and computers, according to Getter. "Real computer literacy doesn't always come with a degree from M.I.T.," he adds; it may be a facility's part-time production assistant or second-string gaffer who turns out to be the staff computer guru. He cautions that "the computer and software market is a jungle and a computer neophyte can become easy prey. A piece of software can look like it does the job, but poor design can limit its practicality."

Getter also warns facilities not to fall into the "gadget happy" trap. He advises them to "make sure that the computer systems you are using really do save you time. A word processor for scripting is a relatively safe bet." After the initial learning period (during which your productivity will be equivalent to using a clay tablet and stone ax, quips Getter), a good deal of time will probably be saved—provided the software is chosen carefully. A database would make a good second application, he adds.

On a final note, the ViMart video manager advises others to keep in mind that it takes a lot of volume to justify handling specific tasks with a computer.

> If your operation is small, it may be better to do things by hand. At ViMart, there are many other things we can do with computers that we have decided not to. The time and expense involved simply would not be justified by the savings.

VISUAL SPECIALTIES
Farmington Hills, MI

Subsidiary of: Financial Business Associates
Type of facility: Production, post-production
Population served: Clients
Micros owned: Apple IIe, Hyperion
Software packages owned: PFS: FILE, PFS: REPORT, Print Shop, Multiplan, Lotus 1-2-3, Blazing Paddles Shapes and Fonts
Contact: Tracy Davis, production manager

The microcomputer primarily used at Visual Specialities is the 256K, 87% IBM-compatible Hyperion; an Apple IIe is tapped for graphics. Both were purchased in 1984.

The Hyperion, which is portable and expandable to 640K, is used for a multitude of studio management tasks, including correspondence, budgeting, personnel records maintenance, inventory control and script generation. It also provides access (via telephone modem) to databases, such as The Source and CompuServe. In all, according to production manager Tracy Davis, the Hyperion cuts by 75% the time spent by Visual Specialties' three-person staff on studio and production management tasks. It has also reduced the "masses of paper" that had been taking over the firm's offices.

Not only is Visual Specialties an avid user of the Hyperion, it is also the system's U.S. distributor. The hardware is manufactured by S.C.I. of Huntsville, AL, a firm that also manufactures shells for IBM computers. The Hyperion, with the Okidata printer and software package, sells for $1750.

For graphics, the firm runs the Baudeville Co.'s (Grand Rapids, MI) Blazing Paddles Shapes and Fonts software on the Apple IIe. Letters can be scrolled, and figures can be manipulated to turn and move across the screen. The software also permits original figures to be drawn.

Davis acknowledges that it is "very hard to find a computer dealer knowledgeable about the television business." She advises others to decide first what the computer will be used for. Then, she says, find the software that will accomplish these tasks; the hardware decision will follow.

Part IV

Appendixes

Appendix A: Microcomputer Survey Questionnaire

Knowledge Industry Publications, Inc.　　　　　White Plains, New York

MICROCOMPUTERS IN TV STUDIOS
SURVEY OF USERS, NOVEMBER 1984

Dear Video Manager,

Thank you for returning our microcomputer survey response card. Please fill out this questionnaire on your studio's use of microcomputers. Information gathered from this survey will be used in a forthcoming book to be published by Knowledge Industry Publications, Inc. Please use additional sheets if necessary.

1. STUDIO
    Name of facility _____ _____
    Parent company if any _____
    Address _____
    Telephone _____ Contact person _____
    Population served (number & type, e.g., general public, company employees, professionals, students) _____
    Type of facility (check one) _____ in-house corporate studio
    　　　　　　　　　　　　　　　_____ production facility
    　　　　　　　　　　　　　　　_____ post-production facility
    　　　　　　　　　　　　　　　_____ cable access center
    　　　　　　　　　　　　　　　_____ broadcast studio
    　　　　　　　　　　　　　　　_____ other (please describe)

2. HARDWARE
    What kind(s) of microcomputer does your facility own? _____
    How many? _____ Year(s) of purchase _____ Purchase price _____

What was included in the purchase price (e.g., peripherals, software)? ____

How much money have you spent to date on hardware, software, etc.?

Micro configuration:
Memory (K) _____ Operating system _____
External storage capacity (K) and type (tape, floppy disk, hard disk) ____

Languages supported _____
Peripherals (e.g., printer) _____
Is the micro connected to other systems via a network? _____
If so, please describe _____

3. APPLICATIONS
   For what applications is the micro used? (Check as many as apply.)
   A. Studio management:
      _____correspondence, memos, reports
      _____budgets and/or financial analysis
      _____personnel records
      _____scheduling and control
      _____productivity management
      _____inventory (small parts, equipment and/or maintenance)
      _____labels and shipping
      _____accounts receivable/payable and billings)
      _____studio catalogs and files
         ____talent
         ____music/sound effects
         ____stock footage
         ____media library
         ____correspondence
      _____electronic mail
      _____security
      _____program logging
      _____CCTV control
      _____other (please describe) _____
   B. Production management
      _____per-production quotes and proposals
      _____per-production budget planning and control
      _____per-production cost analysis
      _____per-production time-line and/or scheduling control
      _____script generation

C. Production tasks:
   _____teleprompting
   _____editing
   _____character generation
   _____graphics
   _____animation
   _____other (please describe) _____
D. Interactive video:
   _____to design an interactive program
   _____to control/present an interactive application
   _____other (please describe) _____
   _____what is the video storage/playback medium?
         _____tape
         _____disc

4. SOFTWARE
   What software packages do you own? _____

   Have you developed your own software? _____ If so, please describe _____

   Do you expect to purchase additional software? _____ If so, for what applications? _____
   Do you expect to develop your own software? _____ If so, for what applications? _____
   Do you have any advice to a studio planning to buy a microcomputer? _____

Please use the space below to describe your facility's experiences with microcomputer use. Feel free to use additional sheets.

Appendix B: Directory of Television Studios Profiled

Aetna Life & Casualty
151 Farmington Ave.
Hartford, CT 06156
Contact: Richard O'Keefe
Phone: (203) 273-3951
Micro: IBM XT

Buick Motor Division
902 E. Hamilton Ave.
Flint, MI 48550
Contact: David Collins
Phone: (313) 236-5147
Micro: IBM PC

CSIU-TV
P.O. Box 213
Lewisburg, PA 17837
Contact: Steve Naugle
Phone: (717) 523-1155
Micro: Apple Macintosh

Deltak, Inc.
1751 Diehl Rd.
Naperville, IL 60566
Contact: Michael Janowski
Phone: (312) 369-3000
Micro: IBM PC

General Foods
Video Center
2500 North St.
White Plains, NY 10625
Contact: Bill Hoppe
Phone: (914) 335-2500
Micro: IBM PC

Hawaiian Electric Co.
P.O. Box 2750
Honolulu, HI 96840
Contact: Scott Shirai
Phone: (808) 548-5670
Micros: Apple II, IBM PC

Hobart Corp.
World Headquarters
Troy, OH 45374
Contact: Paul Hinkelman
Phone: (513) 332-2130
Micros: IBM AT, IBM Displaywriter, Atari 800

IMC Instructional Television Center
Suffolk University
41 Temple St.
Boston, MA 02114
Contact: Bill Walcott
Phone: (617) 723-4700
Micro: Apple IIe

John Stanley Training Programs
208 Charter Oaks Circle
Los Gatos, CA 95030
Contact: John Stanley
Phone: (408) 374-1235
Micro: Apple IIe

KFYR-TV
P.O. Box 1738
Bismarck, ND 58502
Contact: Don Bachmeier
Phone: (701) 223-0900
Micros: IBM PC, IBM XT

Land O'Lakes
P.O. Box 116
Minneapolis, MN 55440
Contact: Dennis Karlstad
Phone: (612) 481-2277
Micros: IBM PC, Apple Macintosh, Magi

LexCom Productions
2720 Sunset Blvd.
West Columbia, SC 29169
Contact: Dale Thomas
Phone: (803) 791-2424
Micro: Sony SMC-70G

Lincoln Center for the Performing Arts
140 W. 65th St.
New York, NY 10023
Contact: Marc Bauman
Phone: (212) 877-1800
Micro: Wang PC

Merck & Co., Inc.
126 E. Lincoln Ave.
Rahway, NJ 07065
Contact: Jeffrey Goldstein
Phone: (201) 574-4067
Micro: IBM PC

Oklahoma Police Department Training Center
800 N. Portland
Oklahoma City, OK 73107
Contact: Dale Bruns
Phone: (405) 946-4407
Micro: Apple IIe

P.A. Bergner & Co.
200 S.W. Adam St.
Peoria, IL 61626
Contact: John Teegarden
Phone: (309) 671-8606
Micro: TRS-80 Model II

The Prudential
2 Prudential Plaza
Newark, NJ 07101
Contact: Richard E. Van Deusen
Phone: (201) 877-7831
Micros: IBM AT, IBM XT, IBM PC, Compaq, Compaq Plus,
    Amqute, Leading Edge

Ralphs Grocery Co.
1100 W. Artesia Blvd.
Compton, CA 90220
Contact: Stephen Brown
Phone: (213) 605-4078
Micro: Commodore 64

Shadyside Hospital
5230 Centre Ave.
Pittsburgh, PA 15232
Contact: Cyril J. Evans
Phone: (412) 622-2716
Micro: Apple IIe

Shooter
3892 S. Mission Parkway
Aurora, CO 80013
Contact: J. Michael Russell
Phone: (303) 699-8200
Micro: Franklin Ace 1000

Sperry Corp.
640 Sperry Way
Salt Lake City, UT 84116
Contact: David Spikes
Phone: (801) 539-7108
Micro: Sperry PC

ViMart Corp.
16795 Lark Ave.
Los Gatos, CA 95030
Contact: Ric Getter
Phone: (408) 395-8778
Micros: Apple IIe, Apple Macintosh, IBM PC, Altos 958

Visual Specialties
27661 Westcott Crescent Circle
Farmington Hills, MI 48108
Contact: Tracy Davis
Phone: (313) 476-4764
Micros: Apple IIe, Hyperion

Glossary

Applications software: Sets of instructions that allow the computer to perform tasks useful to the operator. Designed to carry out a specific function, such as word processing.

BASIC: Acronym for Beginner's All-purpose Symbolic Instruction Code, a computer programming language originally developed at Dartmouth College.

Bit: Contraction of "binary digit" (the smallest unit of information in the binary system); it represents a value of one or zero.

Buffer: Memory that is set aside for special purposes, such as temporary storage of data being sent or received.

Bug: A program error that can cause loss or mishandling of data or a complete crash of the program.

Bus: A circuit that routes data within a computer and out to its peripherals.

Byte: A consecutive group of eight bits, used to represent a number from 0 to 255.

Canned software: Programs written by someone other than the user and available on the software market.

Cathode ray tube (CRT): A computer terminal for data display with a television-like screen.

Central processing unit (CPU): The primary internal section of a computer, consisting of microprocessor chips, memory chips, circuitry and power supply.

Character generator: A device that generates and formats alphanumeric characters and delivers them as NTSC standard video.

Clone: A computer or software program that is nearly identical to a popular model or brand, but is generally available at a lower price.

COBOL: Acronym for COmmon Business Oriented Language, a computer language used primarily in business applications.

Code: Symbols used in representing machine instructions.

CP/M: Digital Research, Inc.'s trade name for an operating system used in many microcomputers.

CPU: *See* central processing unit.

CRT: *See* Cathode ray tube.

Custom software: Programs written by or especially for the user.

Database: Information stored on disk or in computer memory for retrieval and use at a later time.

Debug: To find and correct the errors in a program.

Disk drive: The mechanism used for mass random access storage of data including both the storage medium (hard or floppy disks) and the machinery to spin it at a controlled speed.

Glossary 109

Diskette: Another name for floppy disk.

Disk Operating System (DOS): The disk and memory control system that manages the operations of a computer.

Display screen: Specialized high resolution CRTs that present the results of input after processing.

DOS: *See* Disk Operating System.

Download: To move data from a larger computer system or file to a smaller one.

Edit Decision List (EDL): Time code numbers and other data used by an online editing system to assemble a video program automatically.

Electronic mail: Systems for transmitting data by means of PCs, telephones or wired links to eliminate paper mail.

File: An organized collection of data stored on a disk or in memory.

Floppy disk: A thin, flexible disk of magnetic oxide-coated mylar that is used to store computer programs and data.

FORTRAN: Acronym for FORmula TRANslator, a high-level computer language using algebraic notation and primarily designed for scientific and mathematical applications.

Hard disk: A magnetic oxide-coated disk that is used to store computer data. Usually not removable from the disk drive.

Hardware: Collective term used to identify and classify all the physical components of a computer system.

Input device: A hardware component of the computer system that feeds information into the processor.

Interface: A device that links computers and computer components or peripherals.

Keyboard: A typewriter-like input device, usually equipped with special function and numeric keys, with which data is entered into a computer.

LAN: *See* Local Area Network.

Language: Set of symbols used to denote information.

Laptop computer: A small, portable computer that is usually battery-powered.

Local Area Network (LAN): A group of computers linked by cables, enabling them to share information as well as peripherals.

Machine code: Series of "on" and "off" electrical pulses that are assigned meaning within a computer.

Mainframe computer: A large central computer accessed by many users through individual terminals. Generally available at sizable businesses and institutions.

Memory: Areas within the computer or peripheral pieces of hardware where information is stored.

Menu: A list of functions displayed on a computer screen to enable the operator to make a selection by pressing a key or using a mouse.

Microchip: Collection of very small electronic devices that process electronic data.

Microcomputer: A computer that uses a microprocessor chip as its central processing unit.

Glossary 111

Minicomputer: A physically compact, 32-bit computer that falls between mainframe computers and microcomputers in both size and power.

Modem: Contraction of modulator/demodulator. A device that allows the computer to transmit and receive data over telephone lines.

Mouse: A small unit held in the hand and moved about the work surface to control the location and movement of information shown on the display screen.

MS-DOS: Acronym for Microsoft Corp.'s Microsoft Disk Operating System. *See* Disk Operating System.

NTSC: Acronym for National Television Standards Committee, the body that sets standards for the system of color television used in the United States, hence, the American television standard—including the number of lines per frame and frame rate—is NTSC.

Offline editing: Preliminary post-production session used to produce a rough cut.

Online editing: Final editing session used to produce a master videotape.

Operating system: System software for a particular brand of computer. Operating systems are purchased as an integral part of the processor.

Output device: A hardware component of the computer system that receives information from the processor.

Pascal: A high-level computer programming language.

PC-DOS: Acronym for IBM's Personal Computer Disk Operaing System. *See* DOS.

Pen plotter: Specialized printing device that outputs computer information using ink pens.

Peripheral device: Any hardware device that is not part of the central processing unit, but is connected to a processor, such as a disk storage device or printer.

Personal computer (PC or microcomputer): A self-contained computer system operated and used by a single user. Ordinarily sits on a desk, but can be small enough to fit in a briefcase and operate on battery power.

Printer: A device that creates printed paper copies (hard copies) of the computer output. May be laser-driven.

Processor: The heart of a computer. Made up of microcircuits that process and manipulate information.

Program: The set of instructions used by a computer to perform a task or set of tasks.

RAM: Acronym for Random-Access Memory, usually refers to general-purpose main memory within a computer or peripheral device. Used to store programs and data. Can be erased by the user.

ROM: Acronym for Read-Only Memory, usually refers to circuits that are permanently programmed at the time of manufacture to store programs and data, and that cannot be erased or changed by the user.

Scanner: Input device that can "read" text, bar codes or other specialized markings, or graphics and photographs that exist in paper form.

SEG: Acronym for Special Effects Generator. Also known as a switcher. A device that creates effects transitions between one shot and the next.

Glossary 113

SMPTE time code: The eight-digit address code developed by the Society of Motion Picture and Television Engineers to identify each recorded frame of video by hour, minute, second and frame number.

Software: Directions or instructions that make the computer hardware function.

Spreadsheet program: A program used for budgeting and similar multicolumnar functions that creates the electronic equivalent of an accounting ledger.

Switcher: An informal term for a SEG; any device that routes video from one source to another.

System software: Instructions that allow a computer to start up to do useful work, telling it how to sequence its operations.

Tablet: A sensitized drawing surface connected to a computer as an input device. Comes with a stylus or electronic pen.

Tape drive: An information storage device that uses magnetic tape as the storage medium.

Teleprompter: A device that displays text for on-camera talent to read. Also, the trademark of the Teleprompter Corp. for its version of the device.

Template: Software designed to be used in conjunction with other software to make it more application-specific.

Time code: *See* SMPTE time code.

Transitional language: Instructions for a computer, written in fragmented English.

Turnkey system: A complete system supplied by a single vendor. Includes hardware, software, installation and training.

User friendly: Computer/human interface that is easy to use.

Word processor: A computer program used to write and edit text.

Suggested Reading List

Allen, David. "Sony's New Computer." *Vidcography* (August 1982).

Anderson, Gary H. *Electronic Post-Production: The Film-to-Video Guide.* White Plains, NY: Knowledge Industry Publications, Inc., 1986.

A-Plus for Apple Microcomputing. Published monthly by Ziff-Davis, One Park Ave., New York, NY 10016.

Beer, Martin D. *Microcomputer Interfacing and Associated Programming Techniques.* Dobbs Ferry, NY: Sheridan, 1985.

Brock, Dr. Clifford M. "Teleprompting in BASIC." *EITV* (July 1984).

Budd, John F., Jr. *Corporate Video in Focus.* Englewood Cliffs, NJ: Prentice-Hall, Inc., 1983.

Business Software Magazine. Published monthly by M & T Publishing, 2464 Embarcadero Way, Palo Alto, CA 94303.

Calmus, Lawrence. *The Business Guide to Small Computers.* New York: McGraw-Hill, 1983.

Campbell, Sally. *Microcomputer Software Design: How to Develop Complex Application Programs.* Englewood Cliffs, NJ: Prentice-Hall, 1983.

Computer and Software News. Published weekly by Lebhar-Friedman, 425 Park Ave., New York, NY 10022.

Computer Buyer's Guide and Handbook. Published by Computer Information Publications, Inc., 150 Fifth Ave., New York, NY 10011.

Computer Decisions. Published semimonthly by Hayden Publishing, 10 Mulholland Dr., Hasbrouck Heights, NJ 07662.

Computer Marketing Newsletter. Published monthly by MV Publishing, 1000 Quail, Ste. 120, Newport Beach, CA 92660.

Computerworld. Published weekly by C W Communications, 375 Cochituate Rd., Box 880, Framingham, MA 01701.

Costa, Betty, and Costa, Marie. *Micro Handbook for Small Libraries and Media Centers.* Littleton, CO: Libraries Unlimited, 1983.

Dahmke, Mark. "An Ideal Video Peripheral." *BYTE,* vol. 9, no. 7 (July 1984).

Danhof, Kenneth, and Smith, Carol. *Computing System Fundamentals: An Approach Based on Microcomputers.* Reading, MA: Addison-Wesley, 1981.

Davis, Robert E., Jr. *Selling Your Software: A Beginner's Guide to Developing and Marketing Basic Software.* New York: John Wiley & Sons, 1985.

Degen, Clara: *Understanding and Using Video.* White Plains, NY: Knowledge Industry Publications, Inc., 1985.

Flores, Ivan, and Terry, Christopher. *Microcomputer Systems.* New York: Van Nostrand Reinhold, 1982.

Gayeski, Diane M. *Corporate & Instructional Video.* Englewood Cliffs, NJ: Prentice-Hall, Inc., 1985.

Henderson, Thomas B.; Cobb, Douglas Ford; and Cobb, Gena Berg. *Spreadsheet Software From VisiCalc to 1-2-3.* New York: St. Martin's Press, 1983.

Holland, R.C. *Microcomputers and Their Interfacing.* Elmsford, NY: Pergamon Press, 1984.

Holman, Dr. Neil. "Why Video People Need to Know Computers." *EITV* (June 1983).

Huntley, Joan Sustik. "Writing Scripts by Computer." *EITV* (January 1984).

Icon Review. P.O. Box 2566, Monterey, CA 93942.

InfoWorld. Published weekly by C W Communications, 1060 Marsh Rd., Ste. C-200, Menlo Park, CA 94205.

Interface Age. Published monthly by McPheters, Wolfe and Jones, 16704 Marquardt Ave., Cerritos, CA 90701.

Isshiki, Koichiro R. *Small Business Computers: A Guide to Evaluation and Selection.* Englewood Cliffs, NJ: Prentice-Hall, 1982.

Iuppa, Nicholas V. *A Practical Guide to Interactive Video Design.* White Plains, NY: Knowledge Industry Publications, Inc., 1984.

Jarvis, Stan. "Videodiscs and Computers." *BYTE,* vol. 9, no. 7 (July 1984).
Journal of Microcomputer Applications. Published quarterly by Academic Press, 111 Fifth Ave., New York, NY 10003.
Katzan, Harry, Jr. *Microcomputer Graphics and Programming Techniques.* New York: Van Nostrand Reinhold, 1982.
Kerr, Robert J. "The Word Processor: A TV Production Cost-Saver." *EITV* (June 1983).
Lee, Brian. "Odds, Ends, Over and Out: The Miracle Micro." *AV Video* (December 1984).
The Magazine. P.O. Box 1936, Athen, TX 75751. Apple Macintosh-oriented.
MacUser. P.O. Box 1540, Neptune, NJ 07754-9964.
MacWorld. Published monthly by P C World Communications, 555 DeHaro St., San Francisco, CA 94107.
McPherson, John. "Small Computers Are Versatile Production Tools." *EITV* (January 1984).
McQuillin, Lon. *Computers in Video Production.* White Plains, NY: Knowledge Industry Publications, Inc., 1986.
McWilliams, Peter A. *The Personal Computer Book.* Los Angeles, CA: Prelude Press, 1983.
———. *The Personal Computer in Business Book.* Los Angeles, CA: Prelude Press, 1983.
Micro. Published monthly by Micro Ink, 10 Northern Blvd., Amherst, NH 03031.
Microcomputer Applications. Published 3 times/year by Acta Press, Box 2481, Anaheim, CA 92804.
Microcomputer Digest. Published 11 times/year by C E O Associates, 201 Rte. 516, Old Bridge, NJ 08857.
Microcomputer Review Published 3 times/year by G M L Corp., 594 Marrett Rd., Lexington, MA 02173.
Micro Marketworld. Published semimonthly by C W Communications, 375 Cochituate Rd., Box 880, Framingham, MA 01701.
Milliot, Jim. *Micros at Work.* White Plains, NY: Knowledge Industry Publications, Inc., 1985.
Myers, Roy E. *Microcomputer Graphics.* Reading, MA: Addison-Wesley, 1984.
Nibble Mac. 45 Winthrop St., Concord, MA 01742-9990.
Ogdin, Carol A. *Microcomputer Management and Programming.* Englewood Cliffs, NJ: Prentice-Hall, 1980.

PC Magazine. P.O. Box 2442, Boulder, CO 80321.
P C World. Published monthly by P C World Communications, 555 DeHaro St., San Francisco, CA 94107.
Personal Computing Plus. Published monthly by Hayden Publishing, 10 Mulholland Dr., Hasbrouck Heights, NJ 07604.
Personal Publishing. P.O. Box 390, Itasca, IL 60143.
Prague, Cary N. *Micro Business Graphics.* Blue Ridge Summit, PA: TAB Books, 1985.
Randall, Robert. *Microcomputers in Small Businesses: How to Select and Implement Microcomputer Hardware in Your Small Business.* Englewood Cliffs, NJ: Prentice-Hall, 1983.
Rodwell, Peter. *The Personal Computer Handbook: An Illustrated Guide to Choosing and Using Your Micro.* Woodbury, NY: Barron's, 1983.
Stevens, Richard. *Understanding Computers: A User-Friendly Guide.* Oxford: Oxford University Press, 1986.
Sullivan, David R. et al. *Computing Today: Microcomputer Concepts.* Boston, MA: Houghton-Mifflin, 1984.
Unix/World. P.O. Box 1929, Marion, OH 43306.
Van Deusen, Richard E. *Practical AV/Video Budgeting.* White Plains, NY: Knowledge Industry Publications, Inc., 1984.
Veit, Stanley S. *Using Microcomputers in Business.* Hasbrouck Heights, NJ: Hayden Books, 1981.
Vince, John. *Dictionary of Computer Graphics.* White Plains, NY: Knowledge Industry Publications, Inc., 1984.
Webster, Tony. *Microcomputer Buyers' Guide.* New York: McGraw-Hill, 1984.
Wilcox, Russell E. *Computer and Microcomputer Systems for Small Businesses.* Phoenix, AZ: Oryx Press, 1984.
Wilson, Rich. "Scriptwriting by Computer." *Video Systems* (October 1984).

Index

Ace Calc, 86
Ace Writer, 86
Aetna Life & Casualty, 43, 47-48
   and Satellite Business Systems, 43
Altos 958, 90
Amqute, 77
Apple, 29, 30, 32
   Apple Graphics, 59
   Apple Macintosh, 30, 51, 68, 90
   Apple II, 30, 59
   Apple IIc, 30
   Apple IIe, 30, 64, 65, 75, 84, 90, 93
   Apple II+, 30
   Appleworks, 65
   Apple Writer, 43, 75
   Apple Writer III, 59
   Apple Writer II, 84
Applications software, 7, 12
Associate Producer, 73
Atari 800, 60

Bachmeier, Don, 67
BASIC, 6
Bauman, Marc, 55, 71, 72
Blazing Paddles Shapes and Fonts, 93
The Bottom Line, 55

Brown, Stephen, 37, 82, 83
Bruns, Dale, 75
Buick Motor Division, 49-50

Calc Result, 37, 82
Character generation, 26, 38
Chyron VP-1, 26, 38
COBOL, 6
Collins, David, 49, 50
Commodore, 32
   Commodore 64, 82
Compaq, 77
   Compaq Plus, 77
Comprehensive PowerScript, 84
Comprehensive Video Supply Corp., 35
Computers
   and the media, 13-14
   applications of, 13-21
      See also Media applications
   expansion of systems, 22
   functions, 5
   hardware, 7-11
   languages, 5-6
   memory, 6, 8
   selection and purchase of, 21
   software, 11-13
   system assembly, 24-26
   types of systems, 6-7

Condor, 90
The Consultant, 82
CPM Operating System, 70
Critical Path, 18
Cross Talk, 73
CSIU-TV, 51

Database software, 16-17
DataEase, 55, 77
Data Fax, 73
Davis, Tracy, 93
dBase, 88
dBase III, 49, 60, 67, 88
dBase II, 43, 52, 71
DB Master, 64
Deltak, Inc., 52-54
Dicomed PC Presenter, 77
Dicomed Presenter, 68
Disks
　floppy disks, 11
　hard disks, 11
Displaywriter, 59
Displaywrite 2, 47, 60
Document software, 12-13

Evans, Cyril J., 84, 85
ExecuVision, 52

Flexible disks. *See* Floppy disks
Floppy disks, 11
Fortran, 6
4 in One, 65
Franklin, 32
　Franklin Ace 1000, 86

GANTT, 18
General Foods, 55-58
Getter, Ric, 43, 90, 91, 92
Goldstein, Jeffrey, 73, 74
Graphics Department, 65

Hard disks, 11
Hardware, 7-11, 23, 27
　input devices, 8-9
　memory devices, 10
　modems, 10-11
　output devices, 9-10
　See also Computers
Hawaiian Electric Co., 59
Hinkelman, Paul, 60, 62, 63
Hobart Corp., 60-63
Home Accountant, 86
Hoppe, Bill, 55, 56, 58
Hyperion, 93

IBM, 29, 30, 32, 43
　and Satellite Business Systems, 43
　IBM AT, 30, 60, 77
　IBM Displaywriter, 60
　IBM PC, 30, 49, 52, 55, 59, 67, 68, 77, 90
　IBM XT, 30, 47, 67, 77
IMC Instructional Television Center, 64
Ixion, Inc., 35

Janowski, Michael, 52, 54
John Stanley Training Programs, 43, 65-66

Karlstad, Dennis, 68, 69
KFYR-TV, 67

Land O'Lakes, 68-69
The Leading Edge, 73, 77
Letter Writer, 70
LexCom Productions, 70
Lincoln Center for the Performing Arts, 71-72
Lotus 1-2-3, 43, 47, 49, 52, 55, 60, 67, 71, 73, 77, 88, 93

Index

MacPaint, 51, 68
MacWrite, 51, 68
Magi, 68
Magic Office System, 86
Mail List, 70
Mainframes, 6-7
Media applications,
   accounts receivable/payable and billings, 17-18
   departmental capital, personnel and expense budgets, 16-17
   edit decision lists (EDLs), 19
   equipment and maintenance inventory, 20
   filing and retention, 16
   general business, 13
   general correspondence, memos and reports, 15
   internal/external communication, 17
   labels and shipping, 20
   media control, 14
   music/effects/stock footage, 19
   parts inventory, 20
   personnel and training records, 17
   planning, 18
   production budget planning and control, 18
   production cost analysis, 19
   production quotes and proposals, 18
   production time line and scheduling control, 18-19
   productivity measurement, 17
   program logging and/or CCTV control, 20
   scheduling and control, 16
   script generation, 15
   security, 20-21
   specific production, 13-14
   talent file, 19
Memory, 8
   random access memory (RAM), 8, 10, 11
   read-only memory (ROM), 8
   See also Computers
Merck & Co., Inc., 73-74
Microchips, 3-4
Microcomputer applications, 26-27, 33-40
   general management, 33
   interactive video, 26, 38-40, 45
   production and post-production, 26, 38, 45
      animation, 38
      character generation, 38
      graphics, 38, 45
      teleprompting and editing, 38, 45
   production management, 26, 35-38
      budget planning and control, 26, 35, 45
      cost analysis, 35
      quote and proposal writing, 35
      script generation, 26, 35
      time line/scheduling control, 26, 35
   studio management, 26, 33
      budgeting and financial analysis, 33
      correspondence, memos and reports, 33
      inventorying, 33
      labeling and shipping, 33
      maintaining personnel records, 33
      scheduling and control, 33
      studio cataloging and filing, 33

tracking accounts receivable/
    payable, 33
Microcomputers
  and increased productivity, 27
  and staff training, 27
  applications. *See* Microcomputer
    applications
  expansion of systems, 30
  future of, 45
  hardware, 27
  installation of, 27
  obsolescence of, 32
  ownership of, 29-32
  product reliability, 32
  software, 27, 40-44
Microsoft BASIC, 90
Microsoft Chart, 68
Microsoft Disk Operating System
  (MS-DOS), 12
MS-DOS. *See* Microsoft Disk
  Operating System
MultiMate, 43, 47, 67, 77
Multiplan, 43, 51, 67, 76, 90, 93

Naugle, Steve, 51

O'Keefe, Richard, 47, 48
Oklahoma Police Department
  Training Center, 75

P. A. Bergner & Co., 76
PaperClip, 82
PC CALC, 88
PC FILE, 88
PC FILE III, 67
PC WRITE, 88
Personal computer (PC), 7, 10, 13-21
Personal Financier, 86
PERT, 18
PFS: FILE, 43, 75, 84, 86, 93
PFS: GRAPH, 86

PFS: REPORT, 84, 86, 93
PictureIt, 88
PowerScript, 35
Print Shop, 93
The Prudential, 77-81

Radio Shack, 32
Ralphs Grocery Co., 37, 82
RAM. *See* Random access memory
Random access memory (RAM), 8, 10, 11
R:Base 5000, 77
Read-only memory (ROM), 8
Record Management, 70
Reportpack, 60
ROM. *See* Read-only memory
Russell, J. Michael, 86, 87

Satellite Business Systems, 43
  See also Aetna Life & Casualty;
    IBM
Screen Writer, 64
Scripsit, 76
Script Master, 35
Shadyside Hospital, 84
Shared-time computer system, 7
Shirai, Scott, 59
Shooter, 86-87
Smartcom, 47
SMPTE time code, 43
Software, 7, 11-13, 23
  applications software, 7, 12, 27
  document software, 12-13
  system software, 7, 12
  See also Computers
Sony, 32
  Sony SMC-70G, 70
Sperry Corp., 88-89
Sperry PCs, 88
Spikes, David, 88
Split/Scripter, 35
Spreadsheet programs, 16-17, 18-19, 26, 35

Index

Stand-alone computer, 7
   See also Personal computer (PC)
Stanley, John, 65, 66
Sullivan, Liza, 66
SuperCalc, 70
Symphony, 68
System software, 12

Teegarden, John, 76
Templates, 44
   See also Microcomputers,
      software
Textpack, 60
Thomas, Dale, 70
Titlewriter, 68

TRS-80 Model II, 76

Van Deusen, Richard E., 77, 78, 81
Vendor support, 24-25, 26, 38, 45
ViMart, 43, 90-92
VisiCalc, 43, 76
VisiCalc Advanced, 52
Visual Specialties, 93

Walcott, Bill, 64, 66
Wang PCs, 71
Wang Word Processing, 71
Word processing, 33, 45
   software programs, 15-16, 26,
      33, 35
WordStar, 43, 49, 59, 88, 90

About the Authors

Judith Stokes is a former editor of *Video Manager* and has been a writer specializing in professional video for seven years. She is currently working on a freelance basis. Before joining the staff of Knowledge Industry Publications, Inc., Ms. Stokes was an editor at C.S. Tepfer Publishing Co., Inc. She received a B.S. in newspaper journalism from Syracuse University.

William C. Hight has been working at AT&T Resource Management for over 10 years. He is also involved in both Video Expo and the North American Television Institute, speaking on video facility management.

Software of Related Interest
Available from Knowledge Industry Publications, Inc.

PowerScript™, a word-processing program with automatic formatter. Includes a 5¼-inch floppy disk and scriptwriting and reference manuals.
- IBM PC or XT (128K) $399.00
- Apple IIc or IIe (with 128K) $349.00
- Apple II or IIe (with 64K) $299.00

The Associate Producer™ by Lon McQuillin, a package of production management programs. Includes a 5¼-inch floppy disk and manual.
- AP-A for Apple II, II+, IIc computers $499.00
- AP-B for IBM PC and compatible computers with MS-DOS 2.0 ..... $549.00
- AP-C for Kaypro, Morrow, Osborne, Sony, and TeleVideo with CP/M .. $549.00

The Edit Lister™ by Lon McQuillin, for compiling, managing and transferring an edit decision list with a PC. Includes the E-LINK module, SOFT-SCRUB MODULE, a manual and keyboard reference strip.

With this program, edit lists can be compiled either on a control track system (using window dubs), or by transmitting information directly from an off-line editing controller with an RS-232 output, such as the Paltex ARB-1, EECO IVES, CONVERGENCE ECS-90, JVC VE-92 or 93, and the Sony BVE-800.

The EDIT LISTER (SOFT-SCRUB Module) contains many list management and cleaning features that are currently available only with online computerized editing systems. The EDIT LISTER package includes "E-LINK," a module that allows direct connection to an editing system through an RS-232 edit port.
- EL-A/64SS   APPLE IIe or APPLE II+ with 64K $750.00
- EL-A/128-SS APPLE IIc or APPLE IIe with 128K $800.00
- EL-B-SS   MS-DOS VERSION $850.00

Datafax, a database management program that can handle information in any format. Includes a 5¼-inch floppy disk and manual.
- DF-B   IBM-PC $299.00
- DF-BD   IBM-XT $299.00
- DF-A80   Apple 80 Column $249.00
- DF-A40   Apple 40 Column $249.00

POWERSCRIPT, THE ASSOCIATE PRODUCER, THE EDIT LISTER and DATAFAX are sold by Knowledge Industry Publications, Inc. for Comprehensive Video Supply Corporation. Comprehensive Video Supply Corporation licenses, distributes, and provides the support on this product. No returns accepted. Exchanges will be made for a disk found to be defective. When ordering, list the make and model of your machine.

ALL SOFTWARE PRICES ARE SUBJECT TO CHANGE WITHOUT NOTICE. DISCOUNTS AVAILABLE FOR QUANTITY PURCHASES.

Apple is a registered trademark of Apple Corporation. IBM is a registered trademark of International Business Machines. CMX is a registered trademark of CMX-Orrox. Convergence is a registered trademark of Convergence Corporation. JVC is a registered trademark of JVC Company of America. MS-DOS is a registered trademark of Microsoft Corp. Sony is a registered trademark of Sony Corporation of America.

For more information, or to order, please contact

Knowledge Industry Publications, Inc.
701 Westchester Ave.
White Plains, NY 10604
800-248-5474 (in N.Y. State, 914-328-9157)

PN 1992 .75 .S76

OCT 20 1991